Marxism,
Orientalism,
Cosmopolitanism

Marxism, Orientalism, Cosmopolitanism

Gilbert Achcar

Haymarket Books
Chicago, IL

Ppublished in 2013 by Haymarket Books.
P.O. Box 180165
Chicago, IL 60618
773-583-7884
info@haymarketbooks.org
www.haymarketbooks.org

ISBN: 978-1-60846-364-0

Trade distribution:
In the U.S. through Consortium Book Sales and Distribution, www.cbsd.com
In Canada, Publishers Group Canada, www.pgcbooks.ca

Special discounts are available for bulk purchases by organizations
and institutions. Please contact Haymarket Books for more information
at 773-583-7884 or info@haymarketbooks.org.

This book was published with the generous support of
the Wallace Global Fund and Lannan Foundation.

Printed in Canada by union labor.

Library of Congress CIP Data is available.

1 3 5 7 9 10 8 6 4 2

Contents

Foreword

This book is a collection of four essays, two of which are published here in English for the first time and comprise the largest part of the book. One of the new essays was written especially for this collection; the other has, until now, been published only in German translation.

The first essay, "Religion and Politics Today from a Marxist Perspective", examines Marx's view of religion as a prelude to a comparative assessment of Christian liberation theology and Islamic fundamentalism in the spirit of a Marxian comparative sociology of religions. It was first published in the 2008 edition of the annual journal *Socialist Register*.[1]

The second essay, "Orientalism in Reverse: Post-1979 Trends in French Orientalism", is the text of the fourth Edward Said Memorial Lecture, which I had the honour of delivering at the University of Warwick on 20 November 2007 at the invitation of the Department of English and Comparative Studies. On that occasion I chose to speak on a peculiar instance of "Orientalism" in the Saidian sense with regard to Islam: not the usual denigration informed by a colonial mentality that despises the Muslims, but the reverse attitude of uncritical apology, not only of Islam as a religion but of Islamic fundamentalism itself represented as the *sui generis* path of Muslims to modernity. Both attitudes share a common essentialist assumption of religion as the natural ideology of Muslim peoples, and of secularism as a "Western" ideology alien to them. The essay focuses on French authors because this tradition was born and developed in France, for reasons explained in the text. However, it has certainly spread to the English-speaking world, both in the form of political attitudes paved with good antiracist, anti-Islamophobic intentions and in the form of academic stances widely encountered in the fields of Islamic Studies, anthropology, post-colonial studies, etc. The text of the lecture was first published in the journal *Radical Philosophy* in 2008.[2]

The third essay, "Marx, Engels, and 'Orientalism': On Marx's Epistemological Evolution", was written especially for this collection. It discusses the controversial issue of classifying Marx among the Orientalists in the Saidian sense, begun by Said himself in his famous book. While acknowledging the huge importance of Said's contribution to the debunking of "Orientalist" attitudes, I take as a starting point a criticism of his rather uninformed characterisation of Marx in *Orientalism* in order to examine the evolution of Marx and Engels' attitude towards the Orient. The essay is based on an epistemological appraisal of their thinking in historical context, and pays due attention to its development along with the progress of their own knowledge and experience.

The fourth and last essay in the collection, "Marxism and Cosmopolitanism", was initially written as a long entry in the German *Historical-Critical Dictionary of Marxism* (HKWM) and was published as such in German translation.[3] It begins by assessing the general idea of cosmopolitanism, distinguishing between four general conceptions thereof. It then examines the use of the notion in the writings of Marx and Engels and its evolution, as well the vagaries of its use in the history of Marxism up to contemporary discussions within the broader left, in our era of globalisation.

My thanks go first of all to the editors of each of the three publications mentioned above. In the case of the HKWM, the editors' input went beyond mere copy-editing/translating into a fruitful exchange on the topic. I am also very grateful to my good friend Michael Löwy, who read and commented on the drafts of three of the four essays included in this collection (except "Orientalism in Reverse"). I am also thankful to another of my good friends, Enzo Traverso, who sent me detailed comments on the draft of the piece on cosmopolitanism. Needless to say, none of those to whom I am indebted for this book bears any responsibility for the views that it expresses.

The two essays that were published previously are here reproduced in their original version, unaltered but for editing improvements.[4] Mitchell Albert, the commissioning editor at Saqi Books, was very helpful in nicely editing all four essays. It is worth noting in this respect that this book is my first ever directly written in English, my third language after Arabic and French.

London, 15 June 2013

Notes

1   "Religion and Politics Today from a Marxist Perspective" in *Global Flashpoints: Reactions to Imperialism and Neoliberalism, Socialist Register 2008*, Halifax (Canada): Fernwood Publishing, New York: Monthly Review Press, and London: Merlin Press, pp. 55–76.

2   "Orientalism in Reverse: Post-1979 Trends in French Orientalism" in *Radical Philosophy*, no. 151, September–October 2008, pp. 20–30.

3   "Kosmopolitismus, moderner" in *Historisch-kritisches Wörterbuch des Marxismus*, 7 II, Berlin: Institut für kritische Theorie (Inkrit), 2010, pp. 1892–1926.

4   For the sake of homogeneity, most references to the works of Karl Marx and Friedrich Engels in this book have been located in their *Collected Works* (see bibliography), designated by the acronym MECW.

Religion and Politics Today
from a Marxian Perspective

We had an excellent history teacher in my penultimate year of high school in Beirut. I still remember listening to him with bated breath as he told us the story of the Russian Revolution. That was in 1967: revolution was in the air, and I had been freshly "converted" to Marxism. Like any good history teacher, ours used to discuss with us various matters of past, present and future, after classes as well as during them.

One of these discussions remains engraved on my memory: a chat during a break about the issue of religion. I can't remember what brought us to this topic, but what I do remember is my deep frustration when the teacher contradicted my youthful Marxist positivism. At that time, I was fully convinced that the progress of science and education would wipe out religion in the twenty-first century. Needless to say, I imagined this century as the outcome of the worldwide triumph of socialist revolution, which I expected to happen during the next few decades.

Our teacher held the view that the continuous material enrichment of society would actually enhance the search for spirituality. If memory serves me right, he quoted approvingly the famous statement attributed to André Malraux, and much discussed since, that the twenty-first century would be "religious".[1]

Was my teacher right after all? Is the present vigour of religious creeds, movements and sects testimony to the religiosity of the twenty-first century? What is beyond doubt is that my own youthful expectation was proved wrong; but I do not concede victory to the opposite view for all that. The truth is that we were *all* proved wrong, as the common assumption of our different expectations was that society in the twenty-first century would be one of abundance. Whether it would be atheistic or religious was a question deriving from that basic assumption. The question under debate could be phrased in the following terms: Does the satisfaction of material needs enhance a (supposed) need of religious spirituality?

We will not know the answer to this last question anytime soon, as the prospect of a world "free from want" is as remote as the prospect of one "free from fear" – the last two of the famous "Four Freedoms" defined by Franklin Roosevelt in 1941 as the pillars of the world to which he aspired. The first of Roosevelt's Freedoms – freedom of speech – has surely expanded greatly, though it is still far from a complete triumph. The second – freedom to "worship God in one's own way" – is no longer chiefly threatened by Stalinist-imposed dogmatic "atheism", as people supposed back in Roosevelt's time, but rather by fanatic-imposed single ways of worshipping God, or any deity for that matter – i.e. by various brands of religious fundamentalism. Nowadays, the freedom that appears to be most wanting and most threatened in major parts of the world is actually the freedom *not* to worship any deity and to live in one's own way. That is surely not progress, but the sign of an ideological regression of historic proportions.

The resilience of religion at the dawn of the fifth century after the "scientific revolution" is an enigma to anyone holding a positivist view of the world, but not for an authentic Marxian understanding, as I have come to realise since my first steps in

Marxist theory. This essay aims not only to provide a clue to the resilience of religion in general, but also to account for the various religious ideologies to which history gives rise at different epochs, and their specificities. For not only did religion survive into our times as part of the "dominant ideology", it is also still producing combative ideologies contesting the prevailing social and/or political conditions. Two of these have received a lot of attention in recent years: Christian liberation theology and Islamic fundamentalism. A comparative assessment of these two phenomena from the standpoint of Marxist theory, enriched by further inputs from the sociology of religions, is a particularly challenging and politically enlightening endeavour, as I hope to establish.

Marx's view of religion

Marx announced the boundaries of his thinking on the issue of religion in the programme he set himself when starting his transition from "Young Hegelian" philosophy to class-struggle radical materialism – which is what we call Marxism. His much-quoted passage on religion in the "Introduction" to *On the Critique of Hegel's Philosophy of Right* is the expression of a decisive moment in the formation of his thought. After having drafted the *Critique* in the summer of 1843 (it remained unpublished during his lifetime), Marx wrote the "Introduction" at the end of the same year and the beginning of the next, and published it in 1844 in the *Deutsch-Französische Jahrbücher*. The fact that he deemed it good enough for publication is telling, as throughout his life Marx displayed a reluctance to publish any theoretical writing with which he was not fully satisfied. Along with his famous "Theses on Feuerbach" written the following year, the 1844 "Introduction" maps out brilliantly his course towards what

Antonio Labriola was to call the "philosophy of praxis".[2] In it, Marx wrote:

> The foundation of irreligious criticism is: The *human being makes religion*; religion does not make the human being. Religion is, indeed, the self-consciousness and self-esteem of the human who has either not yet won through to himself, or has already lost himself again. But the *human* is no abstract being squatting outside the world. The human is *the world of the human* – state, society. This state and this society produce religion, which is an *inverted consciousness of the world*, because they are an *inverted world*. Religion is the general theory of this world, its encyclopaedic compendium, its logic in popular form, its spiritual *point d'honneur*, its enthusiasm, its moral sanction, its solemn complement, and its universal basis of consolation and justification. It is the *fantastic realisation* of the human essence since the *human essence* has not acquired any true reality. The struggle against religion is, therefore, indirectly the struggle against *that world* whose spiritual *aroma* is religion.[3]

Here Marx, after stating one of the key ideas of Ludwig Feuerbach's critique of religion ("The human being makes religion; religion does not make the human being"), draws out the full implication of this statement, reproaching Feuerbach for his inability to do precisely that. The next statement, that "the human is no abstract being squatting outside the world", is a direct rebuff to Feuerbach. Religion is an *"inverted consciousness of the world"* only because the human world itself, i.e. society and the state, is "inverted": it stands on its head, to borrow another metaphor used by Marx in relation to Hegel's dialectics.

Following Feuerbach, and with Christianity mainly in mind,

the young Marx fully acknowledged the psychological (spiritual) role played by religion, alongside its essence as a vulgar "false consciousness": "Religion is the *general theory of this world* ... its logic *in popular form* ... its enthusiasm ... its *universal basis of consolation and justification*." However, if one can find in religion a form of humanism – "*the fantastic realisation of the human essence*" – it is only because "the human essence has not acquired any true reality". Thus, "*the struggle against religion is, therefore, indirectly the struggle against that world whose spiritual aroma is religion.*"

Marx then goes on to develop this insight:

> *Religious* misery is, at one and the same time, the *expression* of real misery and the *protest* against real misery. Religion is the sigh of the oppressed creature, the soul of a heartless world, as well as the spirit of spiritless conditions. It is the *opium* of the people.
>
> To supersede religion [*Die Aufhebung der Religion*] as the *illusory* happiness of the people is to require their *real* happiness. To require that they give up their illusions about their condition is *to require that they give up a condition that necessitates illusions*. The criticism of religion is, therefore, in *embryo,* the *criticism of that vale of tears* of which religion is the *halo*.

Religion is an expression of "*misery*": the sublimated "*expression*" of "*real misery*" as well as "*the protest*" against it. This is a very perceptive statement indeed; however, Marx did not, unfortunately, pursue the "protest" part of it. In the following two sentences, he only emphasised the "expression" dimension. They are Marx's most quoted sentences on religion: "*Religion is the sigh of the oppressed creature, the soul of a heartless world, as well as the spirit of spiritless conditions. It is the opium of the people.*" Had Marx stuck to his initial insight and sought to capture the *incitement dimen-*

sion of religion – as well as its *resignation dimension* designated metaphorically by the soothing power of "opium" – he could have written the last sentence differently, using another metaphor to designate a stimulant: *It is, at one and the same time, the opium and the cocaine of the people.*[4]

If one wants people to "supersede" (*aufheben*) religion in terms of its function as their "*illusory happiness*", it should be in order to achieve "*real happiness*". If one wants people to get rid of "*their illusions about their condition*", it means realising a fundamental change in their real condition, into one that does not need illusions anymore. That is why the criticism of religion leads potentially (provided the "*embryo*" is allowed to develop) to the criticism of "*real misery*", that "*vale of tears of which religion is the halo*". The criticism of religion should, then, lead to the criticism of the human world, i.e. state and society, law and politics. Philosophy, after unmasking the "*holy form*" of human alienation, should strive to unmask its "*unholy*" worldly form.

> It is the immediate *task of philosophy* … to unmask self-estrangement in its *unholy forms* once the *holy form* of human self-estrangement has been unmasked. Thus, the criticism of Heaven turns into the criticism of Earth, the *criticism of religion* into the *criticism of law*, and the *criticism of theology* into the *criticism of politics*.

This line of thought is pursued in the 1845 "Theses on Feuerbach", with its conclusion on revolutionary praxis – "revolutionary, practical-critical, activity".

> Feuerbach starts out from the fact of religious self-estrangement, of the duplication of the world into a religious world and a secular one. His work consists in resolving the

religious world into its secular basis. But that the secular basis lifts off from itself and establishes itself as an independent realm in the clouds can only be explained by the inner strife and intrinsic contradictoriness of this secular basis. The latter must, therefore, itself be both understood in its contradiction and revolutionised in practice. ...

The philosophers have only interpreted the world in various ways; the point, however, is to change it.[5]

Ironically, in roughly the last four decades, two religious movements have striven to "change the world" in a subversive manner, in order to establish their own version of the Kingdom of God, an anteroom of "Heaven" on Earth: Christian liberation theology and Islamic fundamentalism. A revealing clue to their respective natures is to be found in the correlation between the rise of each and the fate of the secular left in their respective areas. Whereas the fate of liberation theology is roughly parallel to that of the secular left in Latin America – where it actually acts, and is perceived, as a component of the left in general – Islamic fundamentalism developed in most Muslim-majority countries as a competitor of, and an alternative to, the left in trying to channel protest against "real misery" and the state and society that are held responsible for it. These opposite correlations – positive in the first case, negative in the second – are indicative of a profound difference between the two historic movements.

Religion and radicalism today: liberation theology

Liberation theology is the main modern embodiment of what Michael Löwy calls the "elective affinity" between Christianity and socialism – aptly drawing on a concept that Max Weber coined and named after one of Goethe's famous novels.[6] More specifically, the "elective affinity" draws together the legacy of original Christianity – a legacy that faded away, allowing Christianity to turn into the institutionalized ideology of existing social domination – and communistic utopianism. "Communistic" is used here as something distinct from the communist doctrines formulated with the advent of industrial capitalism. Weber himself depicted quite well this dimension of original Christianity:

> During the charismatic period of a religion, the perfect disciple must also reject landed property, and the mass of believers is expected to be indifferent toward it. An expression of this indifference is that attenuated form of the charismatic communism of love which apparently existed in the early Christian community of Jerusalem, where the members of the community owned property "as if they did not own it". Such unlimited, unrationalized sharing with needy brothers, which forced the missionaries, especially Paulus, to collect alms abroad for the anti-economic central community, is probably what lies behind that much-discussed tradition, not any allegedly "socialist" organization or communist "collective ownership". Once the eschatological expectations fade, charismatic communism in all its forms declines and retreats into monastic circles, where it becomes the special concern of the exemplary followers of God.[7]

It is this "elective affinity" between Christianity in its charismatic phase and a communistic social programme that explains the ability of Thomas Münzer in the early sixteenth century to formulate in Christian terms a programme that Friedrich Engels described, in 1850, as an "anticipation of communism in fantasy".[8] Engels' description was, however, problematic to the extent that he attributed what he deemed unsuited to the prevailing historical conditions to "fantasy". Although he himself acknowledged the affinity between Münzer's "communism" and original Christianity, he reached an inconsistent conclusion, at once crudely deterministic and oddly idealistic:

> *[T]he chiliastic dream-visions of original Christianity offered a very convenient starting point.* On the other hand, this sally beyond the present and even the future could be nothing but violent and fantastic, and was bound to slide back at its first practical application to within the narrow limits set by the contemporary conditions. ... The anticipation of communism in fantasy became in reality an anticipation of modern bourgeois conditions.[9]

Engels could have found the clue to what he described as "anticipation in fantasy" and "a brilliant anticipation" (*geniale Antizipation*) in the affinity between "the chiliastic dream-visions of original Christianity" and the historical plight of a German peasantry faced with profound upheaval and a severe deterioration of its living conditions. Indeed, for a "historical materialist" to see Münzer's vision as a fantastic anticipation of a future state was a surprising assessment of the social programme of a peasants' uprising. In reality, the various programmatic statements of the German peasants were not a product of "fantasy" but of two basic ingredients combined in different ways.

On one hand, there was the utopian "communistic" inspiration found in original Christianity. On the other, there was what could be described as a "romantic" longing for the ancient Germanic communal property system on the part of peasants con fronted with pauperisation and proletarianisation as a result of the gradual dissolution of medieval society. In the same way, three and a half centuries later the Narodniks expressed the longing of Russian peasants for the *obshchina*. In both cases, these were very specific instances of what Marx and Engels' *Communist Manifesto* characterised as the "reactionary" attempt by "fractions of the middle class" to "roll back the wheel of history".[10] However, as Marx would acknowledge many years later about the Russian case, in such instances where commitment to past social forms means preserving collective property, holding back the wheel of history could give, through a spring effect, a powerful impetus for a major leap forward – theoretically, at least.[11]

The communistic dimension of original Christianity is actually what gives sense to Engels' own assessment of Münzer's programme:

This programme, which was less a compilation of the demands of the plebeians of that day than a brilliant anticipation of the conditions for the emancipation of the proletarian element that had scarcely begun to develop among the plebeians – this programme demanded the immediate establishment of the kingdom of God on Earth, of the prophesied millennium, by *restoring the church to its original status and abolishing all the institutions that conflicted with the purportedly early Christian* but in fact very novel *church*. By the kingdom of God Münzer meant a society with no class differences, no private property and no state authority independent of, and foreign to, the members of society. All the existing authorities, insofar as they refused to submit and join the revolution, were to be overthrown, all work and all property shared in common, and complete equality introduced.[12]

Here again the crude "historical materialism" by which the young Engels tried to abide, thereby attaching the "communist" programme exclusively to the proletariat under capitalism, is all too manifest. What Engels was trying to skip in order to comply with the dogma, although he acknowledged it indirectly, was the fact that 1) there is a recurrent communistic tendency that has appeared in various proletarian protests throughout history;[13] and 2) that this tendency can be readily expressed in Christian terms, due to the affinity between its aspirations and original Christianity. Instead, Engels tried maladroitly to explain Münzer as an instance of "anticipation of communism in fantasy", and the Christian dimension as a mere garb imposed by the historical circumstances.

Although the class struggles of those days were clothed in religious shibboleths, and though the interests, requirements, and demands of the various classes were concealed behind a religious screen, this changed nothing at all and is easily explained by the conditions of the times.

The Middle Ages had developed altogether from the raw. They wiped the old civilisation, the old philosophy, politics and jurisprudence off the slate, to begin anew in everything. The only thing they kept from the shattered old world was Christianity and a number of half-ruined towns divested of all civilisation. As a consequence, just as in every primitive stage of development, the clergy obtained a monopoly in intellectual education and education itself became essentially theological. In the hands of the clergy politics and jurisprudence, much like all other sciences, remained mere branches of theology, and were treated in accordance with the principles prevailing in the latter. Church dogmas were also political axioms, and Bible quotations had the validity of law in any court. Even when a special estate of jurists had begun to take shape, jurisprudence long remained under the patronage of theology. This supremacy of theology in the entire realm of intellectual activity was at the same time an inevitable consequence of the fact that the church was the all-embracing synthesis and the most general sanction of the existing feudal order.

It is clear that under the circumstances all the generally voiced attacks against feudalism, above all the attacks against the church, and all revolutionary social and political doctrines were necessarily also mostly theological heresies. The existing social relations had to be stripped of their halo of sanctity before they could be attacked.[14]

These assertions raise two questions. First, how is it that, beside numerous instances of revolts inspired by religious heresies, several plebeian revolts in the Middle Ages did not produce any specific religious heresy, or were even void of any religious character, let alone a theological one? For instance, that was the case more or less of the 1378 Florentine Revolt of the Ciompi, the 1380 French Revolt of the Maillotins, the 1381 English Peasants' Revolt, the 1382 French Revolt of the Harelle and the fifteenth-century Catalonian Rebellion of the Remences. As a matter of fact, sections of the sixteenth-century German peasants' revolt itself, in the Black Forest and southern Swabia, were initially based on social demands free of any religious coating. Second, how is it that the most socially radical expression of the plebeian revolt of the European Middle Ages – the one led by Münzer – was at the same time one of those most directly linked to a Christian "heresy"?

The answers to these two questions lead to a relativisation of Engels' thesis: the dominance of religious ideology during the Middle Ages was indeed such that one could not expect any *atheistic* ideology to prevail among a significant section of the plebeian masses. In an era when the religious *Weltanschauung* overwhelmed every aspect of thought, the tendency for social dissent to express itself within the boundaries of religious creed was likewise overwhelming. However, this does not mean that "every social and political movement [was constrained] to take on a *theological* form", as Engels put it in his *Ludwig Feuerbach and the End of Classical German Philosophy*.[15] They could very well merely invoke the creed with no pretence of producing a theological doctrine, while concentrating on social issues and demands in a quasi-secular manner – unless a specific interpretation of the creed was particularly conducive to the expression of their aspiration.

Münzer's communistic ideology was the most radical ideology of any of the plebeian protest movements against the medieval society, appearing at a time when the Protestant Reformation was signalling the end of the Middle Ages and the beginning of Early Modern Times. The fact that it took the form of a Christian heresy that advocated "restoring the church to its original status" points not, or not only, to an epochal constraint of religion on thought (Münzer, after all, was a contemporary of Machiavelli), but to the convenience of *one aspect* of historical Christianity for such a communistic programme.

Ernest Belfort Bax, in his remarkable history of the peasants' revolts, summarised the demands put forward by Michael Gaismair, one of the most radical figures of the sixteenth-century German peasants' revolt (Gaismair led the uprising in Tyrol and Salzburg, whose demands included the prohibition of the profession of merchant); he then rightly added: "All this is to a large extent an outcome of the general tendency of medieval communistic thought, with its Biblical colouring, and would-be resuscitation of primitive Christian conditions, or what were believed to have been such."[16] As Bax aptly put it with regard to the German peasants' uprising as a whole: "It was, it is true, primarily a social and economic agitation, but it had a strong religious colouring. *The invocation of Christian doctrine and Biblical sentiments was no mere external flourish, but formed part of the essence of the movement.*"[17]

It is this same "elective affinity" between original Christianity and communistic utopianism that explains why the worldwide wave of left-wing political radicalisation that started in the 1960s (not exactly religious times) could partly take on a Christian dimension – especially in Christian-majority areas in "peripheral" countries where the bulk of the people were poor and downtrodden. This was the case in Latin America above all, a region where radicalisation was boosted from the onset of the 1960s by the Cuban revolution and its socialist-humanistic message. The major difference between this modern wave of radicalisation and the German peasants' movement was that in the Latin American case the Christian brand of communistic utopianism was combined not so much with longing for some past communal forms (though one could find such a dimension among indigenous peoples' movements), but with modern socialist aspirations such as those held by the Cuban revolutionaries and various Marxist movements.

Religion and radicalism today: Islamic fundamentalism

Let us now check the findings of the above discussion against the wave of Islamic fundamentalism that took off in the 1970s. The first important aspect to note is the relative prevalence of religion in most Muslim-majority countries compared to the rest of the world.

The *medieval* features that Engels described in *The Peasant War in Germany* – the fact that "the clergy obtained a monopoly in intellectual education", that "politics and jurisprudence ... remained mere branches of theology, and were treated in accordance with the principles prevailing in the latter", and that jurisprudence "remained under the patronage of theology" – applies literally to the conditions prevailing in most Muslim-majority countries today.

There are many and complex reasons for that. In a nutshell: the tenacity of various survivals of pre-capitalist social formations in large areas of the regions concerned; the fact that Islam was from its inception very much a political and juridical system; the fact that Western colonial-capitalist powers did not want to upset the area's historical survivals and religious ideology, for they made use of them and were also keen on avoiding anything that would make it easier to stir up popular revolts against their domination; the fact that, nevertheless, the obvious contrast between the religion of the foreign colonial power and the locally prevailing religion made the latter a handy instrument for anti-colonial rebellion; the fact that the nationalist bourgeois and petit bourgeois rebellions against Western domination (and against the indigenous ruling classes upon which this domination relied) did not confront the religion of Islam, for the reason just given as well as out of sheer opportunism. (The one major exception to this was the borderline case of Kemalism, which developed in a formerly imperial state and actually aimed to westernise Turkey.)

For all these reasons, the situation in most Muslim-majority countries never went thoroughly beyond the frame of what Engels described for the European Middle Ages. Recent times have even witnessed a dramatic reinforcement of the ideological, social and political prevalence of Islam, spurred by the spectacular resurgence and expansion of Islamic fundamentalism, after some real, albeit limited, progress towards secularisation in previous decades. Various Marxist explanations of this resurgence have been offered.[18] What must be noted here is that Islamic fundamentalism, generally speaking, grew on the decomposing corpse of the progressive movement.

Islamic fundamentalism has been a central feature of what was unmistakably a tremendously regressive historic turn. Beginning in the early 1970s with the demise of radical middle-class nationalism (symbolised by the death of Gamal Abdel-Nasser in 1970 following his 1967 defeat by Israel), reactionary forces using Islam as an ideological banner prevailed in most Muslim-majority countries, fanning the flames of Islamic fundamentalism to incinerate the remnants of the left.

Filling the void created by the downfall of the left, Islamic fundamentalism soon also became the main vector of the most intense opposition to Western domination – a dimension that it incorporated from the start, but which had gone into decline during the "secular" nationalist era. Intense opposition to Western domination prevailed again within Shi'i Islam after the 1979 "Islamic Revolution" in Iran, and regained prominence within Sunni Islam in the early 1990s after armed detachments of militant Sunni Islamic fundamentalists switched from fighting against the Soviet Union to fighting against the United States. This followed the defeat and disintegration of the former, and the latter's subsequent military return to the Middle East.

Thus two main brands of Islamic fundamentalism came to coexist across the vast geographical spread of Muslim-majority countries: one that is collaborationist with Western interests, and another that is hostile to Western interests. The stronghold of the former is the Saudi kingdom, the most fundamentalist/obscurantist of all Islamic states. The stronghold of the anti-Western camp within Shiʿism is the Islamic Republic of Iran, while its present spearhead among Sunnis is al-Qaʿida.

Both the collaborationist and anti-Western forms have in common not only their strict literal adherence to Islamic scriptures and their fundamentalist programme, but also their hostility to the left, notwithstanding circumstantial convergences in some instances.[19]

All brands of Islamic fundamentalism share a common dedication to what can be described basically as a "medieval-reactionary utopia", i.e. an imaginary and mythical project of society that is not turned toward the future but toward the medieval past. All of them seek to re-establish on earth the mythicised society and state of early Islamic history. In this, they share a formal premise in common with Christian liberation theology's reference to original Christianity. However, the programme of Islamic fundamentalists is not a set of idealistic principles of "communism of love", stemming from an oppressed community of the poor living on the fringes of their society whose founder was put to death atrociously by the powers that be, as is the case for original Christianity. Nor is it based on some ancient form of communal property, as was the case in part for the sixteenth-century German peasants' uprising. Islamic fundamentalists share a common dedication to the implementation of a once "really existing", albeit mythologised, social and political medieval model of class rule, founded little less than fourteen centuries ago, the founder of which – a merchant turned prophet, warlord and founder of state and empire – died at the peak of his political power.

As is the case with any attempt to restore a centuries-old class society and polity, the project of Islamic fundamentalism amounts necessarily to a "reactionary utopia". By no stretch of the imagination could "*restoring Islam to its original status and abolishing all the institutions that conflict with the purportedly early Islam"* (to adapt Engels' description of Münzer's programme) lead to "*a society with no class differences, no private property and no state authority independent of, and foreign to, the members of society*". It could only mean a huge historical regression.

In light of the previous discussion about Christianity, a question naturally arises: Is there an "elective affinity" between what we will define here as Ultra-Orthodox Islam – characterised by strict allegiance to the *Shari'a* – and "medieval-reactionary utopianism" that would help to explain the way in which Islamic fundamentalism has swept through Muslim communities in our epoch? There are several reasons for arguing that it is indeed the case. Ultra-Orthodox Islam, presently the overwhelming current within the Islamic religion with the backing of the Saudi kingdom, is conducive to religious literalism by its unequalled cult of the scriptures, especially the Qur'an, deemed God's final word.[20] What in most other religions is nowadays the preserve of "fundamentalism" as a minority current – basically a doctrine advocating the implementation of a literal interpretation of religious scriptures – plays a pervasive role within mainstream institutional Islam. Due to the specific historical content of the scriptures that it tries to stick to, Ultra-Orthodox Islam is conducive in particular to fundamentalist doctrines that regard the faithful implementation of the religion as involving a government based on Islam, since the Prophet of Islam fought bitterly to establish such a state. For the same reason, Ultra-Orthodox Islam is particularly conducive to the armed fight against non-Islamic domination, drawing on Islam's history of war against other creeds for its expansion.[21]

For a Marxian comparative sociology of religions

To acknowledge this "elective affinity" between Ultra-Orthodox Islam and medieval-reactionary utopianism, after having emphasised the "elective affinity" between original Christianity and communistic utopianism, does not stem from any value judgement. It is based on elements of a comparative historical sociology of both religions, in the tradition of Marx and Engels, and the late Maxime Rodinson, the most prominent contributor to a Marxian analysis of Islam.[22] A comprehensive Marxian comparative historical sociology of religions, on the scale of Max Weber's famous one at the very least, is still badly needed. Although there have been modest attempts to engage in such a project,[23] for which there are many interesting insights to be found in the writings of Marx and especially Engels, as well as in Max Weber's own deep and rich materialistic analyses, it is a demanding project that remains unaccomplished and must necessarily be a collective undertaking in order to be properly achieved. The different "affinities" peculiar to each religious corpus are rooted in the peculiarities of the historical development of each religion, especially each religion's historical genesis, notwithstanding their ulterior convergence as institutionalised ideologies of class domination. Weber put it correctly:

> It is true that the great ecclesiastic religions differ greatly, especially during their early stages, in their structure of domination and their basic ethics, as it is expressed in rules of conduct. Thus, Islam developed out of a charismatic community of warriors led by the militant prophet and his successors; it accepted the commandment of the forcible subjection of the infidels, glorified heroism, and promised sensual pleasures in the here and the hereafter to the fighter for

the true faith. Conversely, Buddhism grew out of a community of sages and ascetics who sought individual salvation not only from the sinful social order and individual sin but from life itself. Judaism developed out of a hierocratic and bourgeois community that was led by prophets, priests and, eventually, theologically trained intellectuals; it completely disregarded the hereafter, and strove for the reestablishment of its secular nation state, and also for bourgeois well-being through conformity with a casuist law. Finally, Christianity grew out of the community of participants in the mystical Christ cult of the Lord's Supper; initially, this community was filled with eschatological hopes for a divine universal kingdom, rejected all force and was indifferent to the social order, whose end appeared imminent; it was guided charismatically by prophets and hierocratically by officials. But these very different beginnings, which were bound to result in different attitudes toward the economic order, and the equally different historical fates of these religions did not prevent the hierocracies from exerting rather similar influences on social and economic life. These influences corresponded to the universally similar preconditions of hierocracy, which assert themselves once the charismatic heroic age of a religion has passed and the adaptation to everyday life has been made.[24]

Furthermore, to acknowledge the different "elective affinities" found in Christianity and Islam does not mean that there are no countervailing tendencies in each of them. Thus Christianity has included from its inception countervailing tendencies,[25] to which the subsequent development of the church as an oppressive medieval institution added a huge corpus and a very powerful tradition, nurturing various brands of reactionary Christian doctrine and Christian fundamentalism. Conversely, the Islamic scriptures include a few egalitarian leftovers of the period during which the first Muslims were an oppressed community, which have been used for attempts at devising "socialist" versions of Islam.

Besides, the fact that there are different "elective affinities" in Christianity and Islam does not mean that the actual historical development of each religion flowed "naturally" along the slope of its specific "elective affinity". It flowed naturally along the actual configuration of the class society with which each religion became interwoven – hugely different from the reality of its social origin in the case of Christianity, less so in the case of Islam. Thus, during several centuries, historical "actually existing" Christianity was less progressive in many regards than historical "actually existing" Islam. And it is in the realm of the same Christian religion, within the same Catholic Church, that nowadays an ongoing bitter fight is taking place between, on the one hand, a dominant and utterly reactionary version represented by the likes of Joseph Ratzinger (the former Pope Benedict XVI) and, on the other hand, the upholders of liberation theology, who were given new impulse by the new left radicalisation in Latin America.

The acknowledgement of the "elective affinity" that exists between Orthodox Islam and medieval-reactionary utopianism bears no relation to what Edward Said described as "Orientalism"[26] – it can only be so in the mind of enthusiasts of what Sadik Jalal al-'Azm aptly described as "Orientalism in Reverse".[27] Acknowledging an "elective affinity" between a modern political ideology and features located within the historical corpus of a religion does not amount to an "essentialist", timeless view of the political uses of this religion. The contrary is actually true. The clearest illustration of that is the aforementioned "elective affinity" between Christianity and socialism: acknowledging it cannot possibly amount, by any stretch of the imagination, to believing that historical Christianity was essentially socialist. The very absurdity of such a proposition shows how far from "essentialism" the discussion of "elective affinities" is in this essay. Likewise, to acknowledge the "elective affinity" between the Islamic corpus and modern-day medieval-reactionary utopianism, in the shape of Islamic fundamentalism, does not in the least amount to believing that historical Islam was essentially fundamentalist — it was definitely not! — or that Muslims are doomed to fall prey to fundamentalism, whatever the historical conditions.

The acknowledgement of the different "elective affinities" of (original) Christianity and (literalist) Islam is one of the clues to understanding the different historical uses of each religion as a banner of protest. This is what Engels tried to explain briefly in one of his very last writings, where he summarised his earlier views on early Christianity:

> The history of early Christianity has notable points of resemblance with the modern working-class movement. Like the latter, Christianity was originally a movement of oppressed people: it first appeared as the religion of slaves and freedmen, of poor people deprived of all rights, of peoples subjugated or dispersed by Rome. Both Christianity and the workers' socialism preach forthcoming salvation from bondage and misery; Christianity places this salvation in a life beyond, after death, in heaven; socialism places it in this world, in a transformation of society. Both are persecuted and subjected to harassment, their adherents are ostracised and made the objects of exceptional laws, the ones as enemies of the human race, the others as enemies of the state, enemies of religion, the family, the social order. ...
>
> The parallel between the two historical phenomena becomes perfectly obvious as early as the Middle Ages in the first risings

of the oppressed peasants and particularly of the town plebeians. These risings, like all mass movements of the Middle Ages, were bound to wear the mask of religion and appeared as the restoration of early Christianity from spreading degeneration.[28]

At this point, Engels added the following interesting long footnote about Islam, containing insights that bear a striking resemblance to the famous theories of the fourteenth-century Muslim Arab historian Ibn Khaldun, while ending with a reiteration of the reductionist "flag and mask" thesis about the use of Christianity in social protests:

A peculiar counterpart to this was the religious risings in the Mohammedan world, particularly in Africa. Islam is a religion adapted to Orientals, especially Arabs, i.e., on the one hand to townsmen engaged in trade and industry, on the other to nomadic Bedouins. Therein lies, however, the embryo of a periodically recurring collision. The townspeople grow rich, luxurious and lax in observing the "law". The Bedouins, poor and hence of strict morals, contemplate with envy and covetousness these riches and pleasures. Then they unite under a prophet, a Mahdi, to chastise the apostates and restore the observation of the ritual and the true faith and to appropriate in recompense the treasures of the renegades. In a hundred years they are naturally in the same position as the renegades were: a new purge of the faith is required, a new Mahdi arises and the game starts again from the beginning. That is what happened from the campaigns of conquest by the African Almoravids and Almohads in Spain to the last Mahdi of Khartoum who so successfully thwarted the English. It happened in the same way or similarly with the risings in Persia and other Mohammedan countries. All these movements are couched in religion but they have their source in economic causes; and yet, even when they are victorious, they allow the old economic conditions to persist untouched. So the old situation remains unchanged and the collision recurs periodically. In the popular risings of the Christian West, on the contrary, the religious disguise is only a flag and a mask for attacks on an economic order which is becoming antiquated. This is finally overthrown, a new one arises and the world progresses.[29]

The awareness of the different "elective affinities" of each religion allows us to understand likewise why Christian liberation theology could become such an important component of the left in Latin America, while all attempts at producing an Islamic version of the same remained marginal. It also helps us to understand why Islamic fundamentalism could gain such a huge importance nowadays among Muslim communities, and why it came to supersede the left so successfully in embodying the rejection of Western domination, even though on reactionary social terms. In particular, the acknowledgement of the "elective affinity" between literalist Islam and medieval-reactionary utopianism gives one reason for the dynamic expansion of Islamic fundamentalism in modern times, one reason for what Abdelwahab Meddeb called "the malady of Islam".[30]

Other, historical, reasons for the expansion of fundamentalism in Muslim-majority countries have been described at some length elsewhere.[31] They fall basically under four headings: the defeat of middle-class nationalism and the shortcomings of the radical left; the fact that Islamic fundamentalism had been promoted for years as an alternative to the left by the Saudi kingdom and its US sponsor; the ever-increasing exacerbation of the economic, social and political crisis in the "broader Middle East"; the worldwide anomie resulting from both the neoliberal offensive and the collapse of Soviet "communism". To that should be added more circumstantial factors, such as the boosting power of the Iranian "Islamic Revolution" and the Soviet defeat in the Afghan war at the hand of Islamic fundamentalists, as well as the huge impetus given to Islamic fundamentalism by the US aggressions in the "broader Middle East" and the Israeli repression of the "second intifada".

The superficial Orientalist impression, now widespread, according to which Islamic fundamentalism is the "natural" ahistorical inclination of the Muslim peoples is sheer nonsense, of course. It overlooks elementary historical facts. As I have recently written,

> Many people in the West don't understand that there is nothing "natural" or ahistorical in the fact that Islamic fundamentalism is nowadays the most visible political current among Muslim peoples. They ignore or forget that the picture was completely different in other historical periods of our contemporary history – that, for instance, a few decades ago the largest nongoverning communist party in the world, a party officially referring therefore to an atheistic doctrine, was in the country with the largest Muslim population: Indonesia – of course, until the party was crushed in a bloodbath at the hands of the US-backed Indonesian military starting in 1965. They ignore or forget, to give another example of the same kind, that in the late 1950s and early 1960s, the most massive political organization in Iraq, especially among the Shiites in Southern Iraq, was not led by some cleric but was here, too, the Communist Party.[32]

To the possible objection that the above only proves that Muslim peoples have to get rid of religion in order to express progressive political views, one needs only to point to the post-World War

Two decades, contemporary with the long boom of global capitalism, during which mass protest in Muslim-majority countries was dominated by radicalising brands of middle-class nationalism that sought an accommodation with religion, fostering its modernisation. Nasser was undoubtedly a sincere believer and practising Muslim, even though he became the fundamentalists' bitterest enemy. The influence he achieved at the peak of his prestige in the Arab countries and beyond remains unequalled.[33]

Political conclusions

If the reductionist "flag and mask" thesis obviously does not hold much water in the case of Christianity, its application to Islamic fundamentalism can also be very misleading politically. Thus, to pretend that movements like Lebanese Hezbollah or Palestinian Hamas are just peculiar expressions of mass social and political protest, using Islam only as a "flag and mask" or merely as a "language", is to understate considerably the very important reactionary limitations imposed on the radicalising potential of their membership, and even their mass following, by their firm adherence to Islamic fundamentalist doctrines.

True, in the same way that it is necessary to locate every use of Islam, as for any other religion, in the concrete social and political conditions where it takes place – hence, making a clear distinction between Islam as the ideological tool of oppressive class-and-gender domination and Islam as the identity marker of an oppressed minority, as in the case of oppressed Muslim immigrant communities in Western countries[34] – it is necessary also to draw distinctions between widely varying and contrasting brands of Islamic fundamentalism. There is a huge difference, for instance, between an organisation like the most reactionary al-Qaʻida, which, in Iraq, waged a bloody war of sectarian extermination along with its fight against US occupation and holds a truly totalitarian conception of society and polity; and a movement such as Hezbollah, which has condemned "political sectarianism" in the course of its fight against Israeli occupation and aggression and, even while considering the "Islamic Republic" of Iran as its supreme earthly model, acknowledges the religious plurality of Lebanon and consequently upholds the principles of parliamentary democracy.[35]

Still, whatever the case, the ideological fight against Islamic fundamentalism – its social, moral and political views, not the basic spiritual tenets of Islam as a religion[36] – should remain for progressives one of their priorities among Muslim communities. In contrast, there is very little matter for objection in the social, moral and political views of Christian liberation theology,[37] whereas the ideological fight against its strictly spiritual component should certainly not be considered a priority – even for hard-line atheists of the radical left.

Notes

1   See Brian Thompson, "The 21st Century Will Be Religious or Will Not Be: Malraux's Controversial Dictum", in *André Malraux Review*, now based at Knoxville: University of Tennessee, vol. 30, nos 1/2, 2001, pp. 110–23.

2   For a discussion of the evolution of Marx's thought at this stage seen from the angle of "proletarian self-emancipation" as the cornerstone of mature "Marxism", see Michael Löwy, *The Theory of Revolution in the Young Marx*, Leiden: Brill, 2003 (reprint: Chicago: Haymarket, 2005). From the same author, an excellent introduction to the topic of "Marxism and Religion" is to be found in the first chapter of his remarkable book on Latin American liberation theology, *The War of Gods: Religion and Politics in Latin America*, London/New York: Verso, 1996, pp. 4–18.

3   This and the following excerpts from the "Introduction" are based on the English translation available on *Marxists Internet Archive* (MIA) at www.marxists.org/archive/marx/works/1843/critique-hpr/intro.htm – modernised and corrected in light of the German original: Karl Marx, *Zur Kritik der Hegelschen Rechtsphilosophie*.

Einleitung, in *Marx Engels Werke*, vol. 1, Berlin: Dietz Verlag, 1956, pp. 378–9. The MIA text is taken from the Cambridge edition, edited by Joseph O'Malley and translated by him and Annette Jolin: Karl Marx, *Critique of Hegel's "Philosophy of Right"*, Cambridge, UK: Cambridge University Press, 1970. This translation is more elegant than the one provided in the *Marx Engels Collected Works* (MECW), vol. 3, p. 175–6.

4   In a previous article on this topic ("Marxists and Religion – Yesterday and Today", trans. Peter Cooper, first posted on *International Viewpoint* at http:// internationalviewpoint.org/spip.php?article622 on 16 March 2005), I used "heroin" as a metaphor for the *incitement dimension* of religion. A friend of mine, who is a medical doctor, has suggested that the relevant metaphor is, rather, "cocaine". Indeed, as cocaine is defined as "a *stimulant* of the central nervous system … giving rise to what has been described as a euphoric sense of happiness and *increased energy*" (Wikipedia, 2009), its metaphoric use seems warranted here – with the obvious limitations of such metaphors in both cases.

5   Theses 4 and 11, in Karl Marx, "Theses on Feuerbach", MECW, vol. 5, pp. 7–8.

6   In Löwy's above-mentioned *The War of Gods*, a major work of Marxist social theory dedicated to liberation theology. The truth is that conflicting "affinities" were to be found very early in the Christian corpus.

7   Max Weber, *Economy and Society*, Guenther Roth and Claus Wittich, eds, vol. 2, Berkeley: University of California Press, 1978, p. 1187.

8   In Frederick Engels, *The Peasant War in Germany* (1850), MECW, vol. 10, p. 415.

9   Ibid. (emphasis added) corrected in light of the German original, Friedrich Engels, *Der deutsche Bauernkrieg*, MEW, vol. 7, Berlin: Dietz Verlag, 1960, p. 346. Engels' tendency to present the Christian dimension in Münzer as a "screen" is the reason for which Michael Löwy prefers the assessment of the leader of the peasant rebellion given by Ernst Bloch in his *Thomas Münzer als Theologe der Revolution* (1921). This last book was never translated into English; the latest German edition was printed in Leipzig by Reclam in 1989.

10 Marx and Engels, *Manifesto of the Communist Party* (1848), MECW, vol. 6, p. 494.

11 "Theoretically speaking, then, the Russian 'rural commune' can preserve itself by developing its basis, the common ownership of land, and by eliminating the principle of private property which it also implies; it can become a *direct point of departure* for the economic system towards which modern society tends …" Marx, "First Draft of Letter to Vera Zasulich" (1881), MECW, vol. 24, p. 354.

12 Engels, *The Peasant War in Germany*, p. 422 (emphasis added).

13 The term "proletariat" by itself indicates a certain continuity: it is derived from the Latin *proletarius* designating in Roman Antiquity members of the lowest of the plebeian classes, who paid no taxes and whose only "wealth" was their children. Hence the origin of the word: *proles*, meaning "offspring".

14 Engels, *The Peasant War in Germany*, pp. 412–13. Engels reiterated the same idea thirty-six years later in his *Ludwig Feuerbach and the End of Classical German Philosophy* (1886), MECW, vol. 26, pp. 394–5.

15 Ibid., p. 395.

16 Ernest Belfort Bax, *The Peasants War in Germany 1525–1526*, London: Swan Sonnenschein & Co, 1899, p. 86.

17   Ibid., p. 33 (emphasis added).

18   For my own contribution to this endeavour, see in particular Gilbert Achcar, "Eleven Theses on the Current Resurgence of Islamic Fundamentalism" (1981) in *Eastern Cauldron: Islam, Afghanistan, Palestine and Iraq in a Marxist Mirror*, New York: Monthly Review Press and London: Pluto Press, 2004, pp. 48–59, and *The Clash of Barbarisms: The Making of the New World Disorder*, London: Saqi, and Boulder: Paradigm Publishers, 2006, ch. 2.

19   Thus the Khomeinists tolerated the left in Iran until they got rid of the monarchy and achieved control over the state: the tragic fate of the Iranian left thereafter is well known.

20   A literal adherence to the letter of the Qur'an leads easily to uses like those of present-day Islamic fundamentalism, as Abdelwahab Meddeb aptly explained: "The Qur'anic letter, if submitted to a literal reading, can resonate in the space delimited by the fundamentalist project: It can respond to one who wants to make it talk within the narrowness of those confines; for it to escape, it needs to be invested with the desire of the interpreter." See *The Malady of Islam*, Cambridge: Basic Books, 2003, p. 6. One of the key tasks that Meddeb set himself in his book is defined from the onset: "We have to recognize exactly where the letter – the Qur'an and tradition – is predisposed to a fundamentalist reading." (p. 3)

21   There are, of course, many other features that derive more or less necessarily from the literal interpretation and dogmatic adherence to Islamic scriptures – too many to be discussed within the limits of this essay.

22   For a good example of reflections based on Marxian comparative historical sociology, see the interview that Rodinson granted me some twenty years ago, "Maxime Rodinson on Islamic Fundamentalism: An Unpublished Interview with Gilbert Achcar", in *Middle East Report*, Washington, no. 233, Winter 2004, pp. 2–4.

23   See Paul N. Siegel, *The Meek and the Militant: Religion and Power Across the World*, London: Zed Press, 1986 (reprint: Chicago: Haymarket, 2004).

24   Weber, *Economy and Society*, vol. 2, p. 1185.

25   For an attempt at showing how oppressive elements contradicting the "proletarian" character of the original Christian message were introduced already by apostles Luke and Paul, see Anton Mayer, *Der zensierte Jesus: Soziologie des Neuen Testament*, Olten: Walter Verlag, 1983.

26   As is well known, Edward Said himself in his famous 1978 work on *Orientalism* bestowed the "Orientalist" label on Marx (and totally ignored Engels, although the latter's writings on the Orient are at least as significant as Marx's, if not more so). For a critique of Said's statements on this issue, see Aijaz Ahmad, *In Theory: Classes, Nations, Literatures*, London: Verso, 1992. [See also my new essay in this collection, "Marx, Engels and 'Orientalism': On Marx's Epistemological Evolution".]

27   Sadik Jalal al-'Azm, "Orientalism and Orientalism in Reverse", *Khamsin 8*, London: Ithaca Press, 1981.

28   Engels, "On the History of Early Christianity" (1894), MECW, vol. 27, pp. 447–8.

29   Ibid., p. 448. On the comparison with Ibn Khaldun, see Nicholas S. Hopkins, "Engels and Ibn Khaldun", *Alif: Journal of Comparative Poetics*, American University in Cairo, no. 10, 1990, pp. 9–18.

30 Meddeb, *The Malady of Islam*, op. cit.

31 See note 16 above.

32 Noam Chomsky and Gilbert Achcar, *Perilous Power: The Middle East and U.S. Foreign Policy*, Stephen Shalom, ed., Boulder: Paradigm Publishers and London: Hamish Hamilton, 2007, p. 213.

33 Despite the analogies drawn between Nasser's clout in the 1960s and that of Lebanese Hezbollah's chief Hassan Nasrallah during the 33-Day War of the summer of 2006, the truth is that Nasser was hugely more important in that he was not only perceived by the tens of millions as a "hero" but also – certainly so – as their leader.

34 I have underscored this difference in most of my writings on Islam. On the immigrant communities' Islam, see Achcar, "Marxists and Religion".

35 For my views on al-Qa'ida, see Achcar, *The Clash of Barbarisms*; on Hezbollah, see Achcar with Michel Warschawski, *The 33-Day War: Israel's War on Hezbollah in Lebanon and its Aftermath*, Boulder: Paradigm Publishers and London: Saqi Books, 2007.

36 My 1981 "Eleven Theses on the Current Resurgence of Islamic Fundamentalism" ended with the assertion that "even in cases where Islamic fundamentalism takes purely reactionary forms, revolutionary socialists must use tactical caution in their fight against it. In particular they must avoid falling into the fundamentalists' trap of fighting about religious issues. ... At the same time [they] must nevertheless declare themselves unequivocally for a *secular* society, which is a basic element of the democratic program. They can play down their atheism, but never their secularism, unless they wish to replace Marx outright with Mohammed!"

37 Even on an issue like that of abortion rights, the ideological struggle can be fought without questioning the spiritual convictions.

Orientalism in Reverse:
Post-1979 Trends in French Orientalism

The years 1978–79 constitute a watershed in Oriental and Islamic Studies, for they witnessed three outstanding events. I refer here to events that occurred on two utterly different and therefore incomparable levels – namely, "History with a capital H" for two of them and the history of ideas for the third – but all three have powerfully impacted the academic field nonetheless.

The events on the general historical level were, first, the uprising of the Iranian masses that unfolded under a clerical leadership in 1978 and culminated in the overthrow of the monarchy in February 1979, followed by the establishment of the "Islamic Republic" soon afterwards; second, the development of the armed Islamic uprising against the left-wing dictatorship in Afghanistan, prompting the invasion of the country by the Soviet Union in December 1979. The third event, situated on the level of intellectual history, was the publication of Edward Said's *Orientalism* in 1978.

These events occurred at a time when Marxism – which, ten years earlier, had become the dominant attraction for youth globally, as well as the most prominent bearer of the values of the Enlightenment and modernity in most of the Islamic world[1] – was facing a major ideological counter-offensive that had gathered momentum in the late 1970s. The main scene of this backlash was France, where a new label of origin, *"les nouveaux philosophes"*, designated a group of intellectuals (many of them formerly radical leftists, especially Maoists) who turned against their previous convictions and became anti-Marxists, displaying equal zeal and peremptoriness in their new faith and evoking considerable media excitement as a result.

A much more sophisticated and therefore much more formidable tributary to the anti-Marxist ideological onslaught, albeit often from left-wing standpoints, also came in the form of critiques such as those of Michel Foucault and was ultimately epitomised by the very successful launching of philosophical postmodernism, with the publication of Jean-François Lyotard's manifesto in 1979.

The aforementioned three events combined remarkably with this anti-Marxist backlash. The Iranian "Islamic Revolution" – which unfurled in the same year 1978 that saw Karol Wojtyła's investiture as Pope John Paul II – signalled the massive return, with a vengeance, of the "opium of the people" that positivist Marxism had relegated quite prematurely to the museum. The Soviet invasion of Afghanistan affected the ideological standing of Moscow, the mecca of "communism", almost as negatively and as powerfully as the invasion of Vietnam affected that of Washington. Meanwhile, Edward Said's most famous book relegated Karl Marx to the hall of shame of Western-centric "Orientalism" – unfairly, in the eyes of several critics who nevertheless subscribed to the book's central thesis.

"Orientalism in reverse"

One of the most astute of those sympathetic critics of Said was the Syrian radical thinker Sadik Jalal al-'Azm, well-known in the Arab world and in the field of Islamic Studies. The English version of his 1981 essay, entitled "Orientalism and Orientalism in Reverse",[2] was based on a much longer one published the same year in Arabic in the form of a little book bearing the same title.[3] Al-'Azm built upon what he described as "one of the most prominent and interesting accomplishments of Said's book": the fact that it laid bare "Orientalism's persistent belief that there exists a radical ontological difference between the natures of the Orient and the Occident".[4]

He pointed, in turn, to the existence in Arab thinking of what he called an "Orientalism in reverse", embodied in two categories. The first, which Said had already identified, consists in reproducing the Orientalists' essentialist dichotomy with inverted values, whereby the Orient or the "Arab mind" – for those concerned were primarily Arab nationalists – are regarded as superior to the West. The second, then a recent phenomenon in Arab countries and the one that interests us here, was depicted by al-'Azm in these terms:

> Under the impact of the Iranian revolutionary process, a revisionist Arab line of political thought has surfaced. Its prominent protagonists are drawn, in the main, from the ranks of the left ... Their central thesis may be summarized as follows: The national salvation so eagerly sought by the Arabs since the Napoleonic occupation of Egypt is to be found neither in secular nationalism (be it radical, conservative or liberal) nor in revolutionary communism, socialism or what have you, but in a return to the authenticity of what they call "popular political Islam".[5]

In the Arabic booklet, al-'Azm continued, with a wealth of quotes to substantiate his claims, to describe and sharply rebut the key features of this syndrome. Retaining his concept of "Orientalism in reverse", I would synthesise in the following six postulates those defining features of this paradigm that can be extended beyond the specific pool of Arab intellectuals that al-'Azm scrutinised:

1. That the Islamic Orient and the West are antithetic: not, or not only, that Oriental peoples are confronting Western imperialism, but that Western ideologies as a whole, including the most critical ones like Marxism, are unsuited to them;
2. That the degree of emancipation of the Orient should not and cannot be measured by Western standards and values, such as democracy, secularism and women's liberation;
3. That the Islamic Orient cannot be grasped with the epistemological tools of Western social sciences and that no analogy with Western phenomena is relevant;
4. That the key motional factor in Islamic history, the primary factor setting Muslim masses in motion, is cultural, i.e. religious, taking precedence over the economic and social/ class factors that condition Western political dynamics;
5. That the only path of Muslim lands toward their renaissance is through Islam. To put it in terms borrowed and adapted from the Catholic Church: for Muslims, "there is no salvation outside Islam";
6. That the movements that raise the banner of the "return to Islam" are not reactionary or regressive as perceived through Western lenses, but rather progressive movements prompted by Western cultural domination.

This pattern of "Orientalism in reverse" was actually quite pervasive in the wake of the 1978–79 events, and spread well beyond the circles of Arab or Muslim-born intellectuals to the core countries of classical Orientalism. It has been particularly prominent on the French Orientalist scene, as I shall try to establish.

In fact, the most famous of left-wing thinkers who succumbed to the sirens of the "Islamic Revolution" is neither a Muslim nor a Middle Easterner, but none other than Michel Foucault, in a well-known episode of his life.[6] It must be said, however, that, read retrospectively, Foucault's analyses of the process of the Iranian Revolution are chiefly arresting because of their great perspicacity about its social and political dynamics – an achievement that is all the more impressive given that this topic surely did not fall within Foucault's area of expertise. The fact remains, nevertheless, that he was fascinated by what he perceived as a quest for "spirituality", and confused what he heard from the relatively liberal Ayatollah Mohammad Kazem Shariatmadari (who later became a fierce opponent of Ayatollah Khomeini) with the truth of the movement – leading him to declare, naively, that the key tenets of democracy are to be found in Shi'i Islam, and that this is what the programme of an "Islamic government" actually meant.[7]

Foucault, however, was not a professional Orientalist. He defended himself unrepentantly, justifying his enthusiasm for the revolt of the Iranian masses and asserting that the clerical government, which he loathed, was not its predetermined outcome and did not delegitimise retrospectively the support that the mass movement deserved. He knew well that, of all people, French intellectuals are inclined to indulgence towards repressive "excesses" of revolutions, for an obvious reason related to the history of their own country and the official cult of the French Revolution, including its Jacobins – a cult that, incidentally, came under attack in the context of the anti-Marxist backlash, most famously by François Furet. Therefore Foucault felt he did not have to be apologetic; but he never attempted again to tread on

such unfamiliar terrain. I mention him only because this peculiar
Foucauldian episode was symptomatic of a pervasive trend.

Post-1979 French Orientalists

My objective here is to sketch the evolution and meanderings of
those among the post-1979 crop of French Orientalists who succumbed to "Orientalism in reverse". In a single essay, of course,
it can only be a sketch; moreover, I have little incentive to de-
vote the time it would take to write an exhaustive account of this
trend. I shall thus, generally, deal merely with the most prominent members of this group, and only with their key publications
on the issue of Islam.

From the very nature of my starting point – al-'Azm's critique
of Arab "Orientalists in reverse" – it is obvious that the paradigm
is far from restricted to French or even Western scholars. It should
be sufficiently clear, therefore, that my intention is definitely not
to return against French or Western "Orientalists in reverse" their
own arguments about the inability of Western minds to understand Muslim minds (except through unreserved empathy).

Let me also make it clear from the onset that classical
Orientalism, in the sense popularised by Edward Said, is far from
extinct in French Islamic studies – not to mention the general
"intellectual" scene, where it is as strong as it has ever been. As
I shall show, there are even shifts between the two paradigms, as
one might expect in the versatile world of the intelligentsia.

Although this essay is devoted to "Orientalism in reverse", it
should by no means be taken as an indication that this particular
focus is my main concern. It is not; yet my opposition to Orientalism proper, and to Western imperialism, does not drive me
in the least to "cover up" for what I deem to be misguided ways

of countering them – especially that the latter may well be quite misleading in their own way.

The post-1979 generation of French scholars in the field of what I will call here "Islamic Studies" (in order not to restrict it to any particular region of the Islamic world) came to maturity in the post-1968 era. Many of them, like many other members of their generation, were marked in their youth by a more or less committed adherence to radical left views. Some of them – again, like many others – eventually abandoned what they came to see as some sort of disease of puberty, a number of them shifting "from the Mao collar to the Rotary Club", to borrow the metaphoric title of a famous pamphlet published by the French radical left-wing gay activist Guy Hocquenghem in 1986, two years before his untimely death.[8] This generation developed its research activity in the period that followed the 1979 "Islamic Revolution" in Iran, which saw a surge of anti-Western Islamic fundamentalism and its upgrade to the rank of major concern for Western powers – France among the most directly affected.

Three key features characterise this post-1968 crop of researchers in Islamic Studies. They were analysed introspectively by one of their most prominent members, Olivier Roy, in a relatively recent debate on French Islamic Studies.[9] First, most members of the post-'68/post-'79 generation belong to the academic fields of political science or political sociology, whereas the previous generation was still mainly rooted in the traditional disciplines of Oriental Studies, such as history, ethnology or philology. In their majority, they dealt with radical Islamic political movements as the obvious theme of the day, a fact that bore a direct relation to their specialisation in politics.

In the post-'68 years, academics in France underwent a sharp drop in status and relative income. Accordingly, as Roy explained euphemistically, the scholars of the new generation had a strong incentive to look for complementary sources of revenue. One way – which constitutes the second feature (not common to all, of course, but extensive enough to be a key feature) – was to become a "consultant" to foreign-affairs and defence institutions – and, for the most prominent "experts" of the group, not only in France. The other way was through the mass media, whether in the form of direct honoraria for the scholars' "expertise" or as a means to increase the sale of their books – intensive mediatisation being the third distinctive feature of present-day researchers on Islam and the Arab world. The same features, indeed, characterise the field of Islamic Studies nowadays in all Western countries.

The last two features – the propensity to sell expertise to governmental institutions, and mediatisation – did not affect every member of the post-1979 crop at the same time. Some of them resisted the temptation, for a while or forever. This accounts for the increasing differentiation that occurred within the group of "Orientalists in reverse" over the years, as I shall explain. When the new paradigm emerged, however, the impact of the defining events I described earlier – the Iranian revolutionary process, the Soviet invasion of Afghanistan and the publication of Said's *Orientalism*, all occurring across a background of anti-Marxist intellectual backlash – prevailed over a sociologically induced political differentiation that was still in its infancy.

French "Orientalism in reverse"

Post-1979 researchers in Islamic Studies were keen on countering "Orientalist" preconceived hostility to the Iranian Revolution because of its Islamic ideology and leadership, as well as "Communist" hostility to the Afghan *mujahideen,* invoking similar reasons and serving to justify the Soviet invasion of Afghanistan.

They were inclined to reject the defamatory depictions of resurgent Islamic fundamentalism that had gathered impressive momentum under the impact of the Iranian Revolution. This led them, therefore, to reject the very label of "fundamentalism" and its rough French equivalent *"intégrisme"* under the pretext that these pertained to Christianity – Protestantism in the first case and Catholicism in the second. The fact that these terms had acquired a much wider sense since their inception and designated a set of features that applied perfectly to the Islamic brand of the similar use of religion did not matter.[10] The most astounding argument they used – astounding for social scientists, that is – was that the movements concerned referred to themselves as *"harakāt islāmiyya"*, where *"islāmiyya"* actually means "Islamic" as distinct from the passive sense of "Muslim". In other words, post-1979 French Orientalists more or less unwittingly subscribed to the pretension of the so-called "Islamists" to hold exclusive rights on the militant interpretation of Islam.[11]

By an amazing paradox, the new crop of researchers in Islamic studies, careful not to incur the disgraceful reproach of falling into "Orientalism" in the derogatory sense, considered that Islamic fundamentalism was irreducible to any Western-originated category; they ended up calling the phenomenon "Islamism", thus restricting it to a phenomenon specific to Islam – adhering by the same token to perfect "Orientalist" logic. They avoided the terms "fundamentalism" and *"intégrisme"* because, so they said, these words were loaded with pejorative meaning. (Actually, they were pejorative only in the eyes of the secular-minded, whether liberal or radical.) However, the term that they used instead, "Islamism", originally designated the Islamic religion as such, as all dictionaries still attest.

The first recorded use of "Islamism" in the new sense occurred in 1979 in an article published in *Le Nouvel Observateur* (12 March) by Habib Boularès, a Tunisian nationalist who had been a member of the cabinet under Habib Bourguiba in 1970–71 and was to join the Tunisian government again under Zine el-Abidine Ben Ali. His assessment of what he called "Islamism" was not apologetic, of course. The term then found its first use in the realm of French scholarly Orientalism under the pen of Jean-François Clément in 1980.[12] Clément was quite unsympathetic to the movements he described. Thus a further paradox is that the term "Islamism" itself, before it became the pet label of the "Orientalists in reverse", was first applied to the new generation of Islamic fundamentalists by authors who despised them. These authors merely wanted to cover, with a single word, the whole spectrum of political currents raising the banner of Islam, from the most progressive to the most fundamentalist/*intégriste* (a term they did not refrain from using). By providing scholarly legitimation to the application of the label "Islamism" to various political movements referring to Islam, many of them violent and fanatical, they contributed to the confusion increasingly fostered by unscrupulous mass media between the religion of Islam and some peculiar and detestable uses made of it.

A major influence on the formation of the new paradigm was the political sociologist Olivier Carré, who was a generational, intellectual and sociological bridge between the previous group of French specialists of the Muslim world (many of whom were truly erudite) and the new crop, who are much shallower overall for the existential reasons indicated, not least among them the ravages of mediatisation. Carré has been far less frequently translated into English than have the prominent members of the post-1979 generation, although he is definitely more learned and interesting. In 1979 he published a scholarly study of the way Arab nationalism – his major focus of interest at that time – used progressive interpretations of Islam for its own legitimation.[13] Dwelling on views he had explored previously, one major hypothesis of his book was that the future emergence of a distinctly Arab progressive Islam was quite possible (a view with which I concur) and that it was, indeed, already in process – a more debatable prognosis in its time, to be sure, and one that has since, in my view, been invalidated by history.[14]

Carré was thus somewhat predisposed to blur the distinctions between Arab nationalism and Islamic fundamentalism. In 1982 he stressed the similarity between what he then started calling "Islamism" and Arab nationalism, which he saw confirmed by Muammar al-Qaddafi – a hybrid of both, as he seemed then.[15] Such a similarity could be emphasised only if one looked at the problem from the angle of discourse analysis, which is chiefly what Carré had been doing. The nationalists needed, naturally, to prevent their opponents from pre-empting Islam, whereas the fundamentalists – particularly in the 1960s, the era of "Arab socialism" – needed to convince the masses that their Islam, too, was "socialist" in some way, hence rebutting the accusation that they intended to bring the old wealthy classes back to power.

In a book published in 1983 – mainly an anthology of texts from the Egyptian and Syrian branches of the Muslim Brotherhood, edited in collaboration with Michel Seurat – Carré went even further, the balance of his sympathies tilting now towards the "Islamists" against the nationalists whom he labelled "totalitarian".[16] In statements typical of "Orientalism in reverse", he now described "political Islam" as "the 'popular culture' of the Muslim world that is managing to express itself at last" after having been muffled successively by colonialism and post-independence regimes;[17] "the despised modern form of ancestral popular culture";[18] and as "a remarkably permanent fact, in its goals and its means, since the dawn of the intrusion of industrial Europe in the Arab world" – a view that correlates with Carré's belief that "religiosity is a permanent and essential phenomenon of Arab societies".[19]

Perhaps Seurat meant to warn against his co-author's drift when he wrote in their joint book: "One should not reverse purely and simply this scheme [of the Muslim Brotherhood's reactionary character] to the point of regarding the Muslim Brotherhood as the new heralds of modernisation".[20] The fact is that this is exactly what Carré did, quite emphatically, in another book published the same year,[21] where he ended the introduction to his contribution with the following imaginative statement by a fictitious "Islamist":

> Reaction, fundamentalism, obscurantism, clericalism, Middle Ages! "Let's be serious," – replies the Islamist militant with bright eyes – "the only, the true progressivism is the Islamic alternative. The only, the true modernisation is the autochthonous modernisation, rooted in our popular culture, and it is Islamic to the fingernails."[22]

Similar statements were made further on in the same book by Carré without using an "Islamist" dummy: thus, he wrote, the "Islamist" current "mobilises for a practice, that is already initiated, of 'autochthonous modernisation' at the local level in immediate harmony with the language of 'popular culture', which is fundamentally Islamic".[23] Such statements include two themes that, combined, were to become distinctive of the French version of the "Orientalism in reverse" paradigm: "Islamism" as an agent of modernisation and the religion of Islam as the essential language and culture of Muslim peoples.

A landmark in the history of the post-1979 crop of French Orientalism came in 1984, with the publication of Gilles Kepel's book on radical fundamentalist groups in post-Nasserite Egypt.[24] Kepel never really adhered to "Orientalism in reverse", but stood halfway between it and traditional Orientalism. His first book actually featured a preface by none other than Bernard Lewis, Said's chief target. Adopting a relatively neutral tone in describing Egyptian radical fundamentalists, Kepel contributed to the confirmation of the "Islamist" label by arguing in its favour in his conclusion. His neutral stance could be seen as warranted by the fact that he dealt mainly with the most fanatical and most violent fringe of Islamic fundamentalism.

On the other hand, Kepel quickly became the most blatant embodiment of all the characteristics of the new generation of Orientalists as described above (including a trajectory that began on the far left). His book displayed a pattern that was to typify all his abundant subsequent production: a wealth of useful information – later facilitated by privileged access to governmental sources – with a limited theoretical conceptualisation that became shallower in book after book. He became a star of the mass media – the Bernard-Henri Lévy of French Orientalism, somehow – as well as an adviser to Western and other governments in their fight against radical Islamic fundamentalism. He ended up actively promoting and defending the ban on the veil in French schools.

One year after Kepel's book on Egypt, another landmark of post-1979 French Orientalism appeared, which contributed to the paradigm of "Orientalism in reverse" in a more direct way: Olivier Roy's book on Afghanistan.[25] A former Maoist, Roy very openly displayed his sympathy for the Afghan Islamic movements as well as his hostility to those he called the "communists". Although he seemed to take heed of Seurat's warning in the introduction to his book,[26] what he actually did was to continue and amplify Carré's elevation of Islamic fundamentalism to the rank of a bearer of modernity.

Roy introduced a distinction between "Islamism" and what he called *"fondamentalisme"*, using the Gallicised version of the

English term rather than *intégrisme*, the label used by those on
the French left who described the Afghan *mujahideen* as reactionary forces, the Afghan equivalent of the French counter-
revolutionary Chouans of the late eighteenth century. In Roy's
lexicon, "fundamentalism" bears the usual meaning: advocacy of
a return to the Holy Scriptures of Islam and strict observance of
the *Shari'a*. He compared Islamic fundamentalism, however, to
the Protestant Reformation instead of comparing it to Protestant
fundamentalism. "Islamism", he clarified, is "fundamentalism"
turned militant and oppositional, especially in an urban context
or in brutally "modernised" societies.[27]

Emphasising "the modernity of Islamism",[28] he then explained
that the Afghan "Islamists", influenced by Egypt's Muslim Brotherhood, were striving "to develop a modern political ideology
based on Islam, which they see as the only way to come to terms
with the modern world ..."[29] He also wrote: "The West (both
liberal and Marxist) is attempting to relegate to the realms of ar-
chaism, feudalism, the Middle Ages and obscurantism ideas that
are, in fact, products of modernism."[30] Furthermore, according to
Roy, "the systematic return to the *Shari'a* creates the conditions
for the advent of a certain form of modernity, political at least"[31]
in allowing for the traditional segmentation of Afghan society to
be superseded by religion as a unifying factor. Leaving aside the
fact that Roy's portrait of the Afghan "Islamists" as transcending
the variegated segmentation of their society was just a fantasy,
this is indeed a kind of "modernisation" that is as old as the emergence of religions, and which Ibn Khaldun already described in
similar terms six hundred years ago.

The third landmark of post-1979 French Orientalism,
completing my selection of prominent figures of this group,
was the publication of François Burgat's book on the Maghreb
in 1988.[32] Among the well-known members of post-1979 French

Orientalism, Burgat is by far the most zealous upholder of "Orientalism in reverse". Building squarely on Carré, whom he described as "one of the undisputed masters of the thinking on political Islam",[33] Burgat's view is best encapsulated in the following quote:

> Expressing the "restoration of cultural balance" that ensues from the forced withdrawal of the West, initiated on the political level with decolonisation and independence and continued on the economic level through nationalisations, the process of disengagement manifests itself nowadays on the cultural level through Islamism. By allowing those who were dominated yesterday to affirm their identity in the face of the West without resorting to precisely the vocabulary that it had imposed, Islamism, from Kabul to Marrakech, partakes of the same need of a return to the cultural roots.[34]

The two key tenets of the paradigm of French "Orientalism in re-verse" as formulated by Carré – namely that "Islamism" is an agent of modernisation and that the religion of Islam is the essential lan-guage and culture of Muslim peoples – found in Burgat their most extreme expression. They combined with a third idea also inspired by Carré, that of the continuity rather than discontinuity between nationalism and "Islamism". It became, for Burgat, continuity between the historical nationalist moment and the resurgence of Islamic fundamentalism. Thus, he wrote, "being a modernising re-sponse to the problems of modernity, Islamism expresses therefore a need for continuity more than for rupture".[35]

This idea of continuity is illustrated by Burgat with the meta-phor of a single rocket of decolonisation with three stages – the first one political (independence), the second economic (nation-alisations) and the third, represented by "Islamism", cultural/

ideological. This metaphor completely disregards the fact that the so-called "Islamism" – in what was actually its resurgence after a long marginalisation – came along with a massive reversal of both political and economic independence: the 1970s saw a comeback of US hegemony in the Muslim world and a foretaste of the worldwide neoliberal regression, best represented by Egypt's "de-Nasserisation" under Anwar al-Sadat. To use Burgat's metaphor, it did not occur to him that the rocket's third stage was actually activated in a phase of descent – in other words, that the spread of Islamic fundamentalism was one expression among others of a tremendous setback and multifarious regression in the Orient's history of decolonisation.

The cornerstone upon which Carré and Burgat's view is based considers "Islamism" only as a matter of discourse, as modernisation expressed in a different language. While the language of the nationalists was borrowed from the West in their view, the language of the "Islamists" is "autochthonous" (to quote Carré's expression again). The ultimate consequence of this conception by Burgat is to reduce "Islamism" to a mere mode of expression – "Muslim speech" (*"le parler musulman"*), as he would call it later – for a programme that is basically the same as that of nationalism. To quote him again:

> Islamism, therefore, is more a language than a doctrine; a way of representing reality that does not content itself with borrowing from what the dominant imposed ... With some exaggeration, one could dissociate Islamism from religion and see in this resorting to the vocabulary of Islam in order to express an alternative political project nothing but the ideological logistics of political independence, the cultural continuation of the ruptures resulting from decolonisation.[36]

One interesting aspect of Burgat's work is that it includes transcripts of talks and other exchanges he had with prominent figures of the "Islamist" scene. As it happens, these are at times more enlightening than his own explanations. Thus the clearest rebuttal to his views was expressed by the famous Moroccan Islamic fundamentalist, Sheikh Abdessalam Yassine, the founder of the association Al-'Adl wal-Ihsān (Justice and Charity), who told Burgat:

> You, the external observers, when you read the literature of the Islamists ... when you analyse their discourse, you only perceive the tip of the iceberg ... that is the denunciation of Western cultural domination ... the denunciation of bad governance, the existence of this social injustice ...
>
> In your articles, I read the analysis of a pure Westerner who sympathises with Islamism ... indeed... you sympathise with Islam. But, for you, this spiritual sphere remains voluntarily opaque. You don't want to see it; you don't want to look at it. In fact, I recognise the failing of those intellectuals who place great emphasis on their own point of view without taking into account that of others."[37]

The meanderings of French "Orientalism in reverse"

Let me now sketch briefly the subsequent evolution of French "Orientalism in reverse". The post-1979 generation of French specialists of the Muslim world was affected by a most tragic event: the 1986 assassination or death in detention of Michel Seurat, who had been abducted in Lebanon the year before by a group calling itself "Islamic Jihad" and suspected of being a façade for

Hezbollah, acting on behalf of Iran.[38] This was a devastating shock for the French Orientalist community, and for Olivier Carré in particular, with whom Seurat had collaborated closely. Consequently, the image of Iran darkened considerably in their eyes, and so did their notion of "Islamism" for most of them.

In the introduction to the first book he published after Seurat's tragic death, a collection of essays that came out in 1991, Carré displayed a very different assessment of so-called "Islamism" in the light of Iran:

> The Iranian example, especially since 1981, diminishes the credibility of the 'Islamist alternative' ... The tragic example of Michel Seurat, with whom I have worked and from whom I draw inspiration, alas confirms remarkably the antagonistic game of the two barbarisms (Islamist and 'secular progressive' [*sic*]) ...[39]

Thus Carré broke radically with "Orientalism in reverse". He reversed it, if I may say so, meaning by this that he went back to Orientalism proper. The latter on the French scene is divided between two schools nowadays, but the same pattern applies to other communities of Orientalists. One was labelled "neo-Orientalism" by Farhad Khosrokhavar,[40] although it is rather a traditional one – to put it roughly, it is the view that Islam is incompatible with modernity. The other I have called "new Orientalism", for it is new indeed and defined as the view that not only are Islam and modernity compatible, but in fact Islam is the only and necessary path to modernity in the Muslim world.[41]

"Orientalism in reverse" shares a common core with traditional Orientalism: the essentialist view according to which "religiosity is a permanent and essential phenomenon" for Muslim peoples, to repeat Carré's already quoted sentence. Breaking with his illusions about "Islamism", Carré, to be sure, did not go as far as rejecting Islam as such. By an obvious instance of wishful thinking, he came to believe that the time of "Islamism" was coming to an end in the Muslim world, and that "the era of post-Islamist compromises seems set out ..."[42] Two years later, he published a very interesting book – regrettably not yet translated into English – where he announced in the title itself the coming of what he called paradoxically "secular Islam", actually a return to what he called "the Great Tradition".[43]

By "Great Tradition", Carré meant the long Islamic tradition established after the tenth century until the emergence of a new Islamic "orthodoxy" in the late nineteenth and early twentieth centuries, based on puritanical interpretations of Islam – those of Ibn Hanbal and Ibn Taymiyyah in particular – that laid the ground for the wave of "Islamism". Carré's remarkable book is a plea for a moderate, relatively secularised Islam, which could almost have been written by an enlightened Muslim scholar. The "new Orientalist" bias nonetheless re-emerged at the opening of the book's conclusion, in which Carré postulated that "secularisation can only be Islamic in Muslim societies and cultures"[44] – in other words, that no thorough separation of religion and state can occur in Muslim lands.

In 1992, Olivier Roy published in turn a book heralding the "failure of political Islam".[45] Reiterating his previous "Orientalist in reverse" assessment that "Islamism" was an agent of modernisation and secularisation, he decreed that this "Islamism" had failed. By a trick typical of the intellectual profession, instead of admitting that this modern and secular "Islamism" was but a figment of his own and his colleagues' imagination – i.e. that the failure was that of his own analysis – Roy attributed it to the object of his study. Now, he wrote:

In retrospect, it appears that the political action of the
Islamists, far from leading to the establishment of Islamic states
or societies, falls in either with the logic of the state (Iran), or
with traditional, if reconfigured, segmentation (Afghanistan).[46]
Islamism was a moment, a fragile synthesis between Islam
and political modernity, which ultimately never took root.[47]

The reason for this alleged failure, according to Roy, is an intellectual impasse (*"aporie"*) in "Islamist" thought whereby virtuous
people are deemed a necessary condition for the establishment of
an Islamic society while an Islamic society is the necessary condition for the education of virtuous people.[48] Leaving aside the
extreme shallowness of such an explanation, the question is how
Roy did not realise the *"aporie"* from the start, which is a failing
he did not even acknowledge. The failure of "revolutionary Islamism" led, said Roy, to its "social-democratisation" – an amazing
import of a concept coming from a person belonging to a group
that rejected the term *"intégrisme"* on the ground that it originated
in the history of another religion. Failed "Islamism" turned into
what Roy called *"néofondamentalisme"* ("neo-fundamentalism"),
i.e. a socially "conservative" interpretation of Islam as opposed to
a "modernising" one – as if this feature had not been at the core
of so-called "Islamism" from the very beginning.

Roy's subsequent book came out in French barely one year after
the 11 September 2001 al-Qaʻida attacks, and was written in the
main before the events.[49] It was thus not primarily a reaction to the
traumatic shock of 9/11 as much as a further stage in the author's
thinking. The English edition came out two years later, translated,
rewritten and augmented by the author himself.[50] It involves, consequently, more references to the defining moment of the Bush
administration's "war on terror", but the bulk of the book nevertheless remains the author's more general attempt at confronting

his previous analyses with a reality that keeps contradicting them. Theoretical confusion is perhaps what explains the fact that the book reads at times more like a nebulous philosophical comment on the state of the world than like a work of social science.

The new development central to this book could be thought of as inspired by Carré, as it deals with "post-Islamism". However, Roy's thesis is that "Islamism" itself has now turned into "post-Islamism" through the "overpoliticisation of religion", which – by the cunning of History – has led to the distancing of the religious sphere from the political, each becoming "autonomous, despite the wishes of the actors" themselves, thus setting "the conditions for secularisation".[51] According to Roy, one major facet of "post-Islamism" is the move of some organisations "from Islamism to nationalism": there is a "blurring of the divide between nationalists and Islamists everywhere in the Arab Middle East", he asserts, with Lebanese Hezbollah and Palestinian Hamas being the key examples in this respect.[52] One illustration of this, wrote Roy in 2004, is that it is "increasingly difficult to distinguish between a Hamas Islamist militant and a supposedly secular member of Arafat's Fatah"[53] – a statement that reads today as an invalidation of his thesis in light of the widening gulf between the two forces.

At any rate, to present Hezbollah and Hamas as signalling a shift "from Islamism to nationalism" and a transformation into new hybrid "Islamo-nationalist" forces is unwarranted for at least two reasons: on the one hand, both have been involved since their inception in a struggle against the foreign occupation of their territory. Such a struggle has never been the monopoly of forces labelled "nationalist" but was always waged in the region, historically, by a broad spectrum of forces within which various religious elements played a prominent role from the initial stages. On the other hand, to "blur" the significance of the "Islamism" of the designated organisations just because they are engaged in the national struggle outbidding their "nationalist" rivals is obviously misleading, as history keeps demonstrating abundantly.

The other major illustration of Roy's thesis on "post-Islamism" is the Iranian "Islamic Republic". His long comments on an alleged "secularisation" and "declericalisation" of the Iranian polity[54] – all the more paradoxical in that it was chiefly epitomised by former President Mohammad Khatami, the "reformist" head of the "Assembly of Militant Clerics" – were based on the illusion that Iran was fulfilling by then (2002–04) its "political normalisation".[55] The Iranian president elected in 2005, Mahmoud Ahmadinejad, was, of course, the living refutation of this peremptory assertion, which was premature at the very least. By another cunning of History, he is a layman.

I could go on discussing most of the assertions in Roy's book, such as "the privatisation of re-Islamisation"[56] illustrated by the Egyptian Muslim Brotherhood and the Pakistani alliance of fundamentalist groups, which Roy believed to be no longer interested in changing the state; the "deterritorialisation" of "Islamism", illustrated by the allegation that al-Qa'ida "has been conspicuously absent from the Middle East"[57] and that it has "hardly ever undertaken missions in the region or with a regional objective",[58] an allegation that was evidently wrong since the emergence of al-Qa'ida in the early 1990s; and the equally wrong assertion that: "if one looks at Islamic radicalisation among young Muslims (and converts) in the West, their background has nothing to do with Middle East conflicts".[59]

The London bombings of 7 July 2005 put this last assertion to the test. Roy hurriedly brought his support to the British government's attempt to deny the obvious connection between Middle East conflicts – principally Britain's participation in the occupation of Iraq – and the attacks. He published an op-ed in *The New York Times* a few days after the bombings, entitled "Why

Do They Hate Us? Not Because of Iraq",[60] wherein he explained that the London bombers were not reacting to US and British wars, but rather saw these wars "as part of a global phenomenon of cultural domination". One year later, during Israel's onslaught against Lebanon, he published an op-ed in *Le Monde* wherein he gave advice to the "Sunni regimes" [*sic*] and Israel on how best to isolate Hezbollah, concluding his article with the following sentence: "More than ever the political way should prevail: this way is not necessarily that of diplomacy, but that of adjusting military force to political ends."[61]

Then, in September 2006, Roy published yet another op-ed in the world press, entitled "We're Winning, Despite the 'War'",[62] explaining that "the world is safer" because of the "protracted mobilization of police, experts, intelligence agencies and judiciaries" (he couldn't possibly omit the "experts"). Thus, in the space of twenty years, Olivier Roy – who had started as an "Orientalist in reverse" – completed his transformation into the kind of "expert" who advises Western governments à la Kepel, a transformation in light of which his introspective analysis of 2001 quoted above seems quite perceptive, though it was meant to be apologetic.

Of our three outstanding "Orientalists in reverse" – Carré, Roy and Burgat – only the third still sticks steadfastly to his earlier views. Indeed, Burgat's subsequent two books on "Islamism" mostly reiterate the same views outlined in the first, even more oversimplified at times if anything, in the heat of the polemics in which he indulged against his former co-thinkers.[63] He conceded, however, that there were reactionary currents within "Islamism", which, incidentally, he did not hesitate to call *"intégristes"*. However, these were only bad apples, which he did not want confused with the whole lot.

The reactionary component of the Islamist recipe is not the only one. The fact that the literalists and the fundamentalists appear condemned to grow and evolve means that no-one should dare to predict if and how Islamism, generally and specifically, will ever adapt or play itself out in terms that we would call "modern" meant as a term to denote a core of universal values.[64]

Burgat, however, did not only engage in polemics against his former fellow "Orientalists in reverse", but also, chiefly and courageously – it should be stressed – against the wave of Islamophobia that engulfed his country in the wake of 9/11. He opposed his government's policies and the dominant trend in the media on issues like the ban on the veil in the schools or the French role in Lebanon. This necessary acknowledgement leads me to the point with which I wish to conclude, going back to where I started from: Sadik Jalal al-'Azm's 1981 essay.

Al-'Azm concluded his article about Arab "Orientalism in reverse" by asserting that the latter "is, in the end, no less reactionary" than "'Orientalism' proper".[65] This kind of assessment is not, and cannot be, universally valid in my view. As for any value judgement, what is assessed should be put in context and evaluated relative to that context. Switching from an Arab context to a Western one, the role of "Orientalism in reverse" changes radically. Whereas in the first instance, it is indeed a capitulation to what amounts to a historical regression of massive proportion, it is often, in the second case, a form of resistance to dominant imperialist ideology and of sympathy with its targets. Burgat is the typical embodiment of such an attitude, which bears a great resemblance to the "Third-Worldism" of yesteryear, which also indulged in self-delusion by falling blindly in love with the enemies of their enemies.

The way Maxime Rodinson described the "Third-Worldist"

approach to Islam in 1968 bears a striking resemblance to what I have discussed above, showing that "Orientalism in reverse" is indeed a recurrent phenomenon:

> The universalism that [leftwing anti-colonialism] derived from its liberal or socialist roots tended to change into a recognition, and ultimately, even an exultation of individuality. Now, it was in the Third World that the exploited, oppressed and brutalized element with its crude strength would, once and for all, overthrow the misery and domination of the old order. From then on, those values intrinsic to the formerly colonized peoples were to receive due praise, which was not diminished even when very normal misunderstandings resulted in perceiving in them, albeit in specific forms, the very same values that animated the European groups concerned. To some of those who were more deeply committed in this direction, Islam itself was seen as an inherently "progressive" force.[66]

Still, between "experts" advising Western governments on the conduct of their imperial policies and "Orientalists in reverse" denouncing this same conduct – albeit with huge illusions about those targeted by these policies, thus preparing the way for the disillusionments of tomorrow and their demoralising effect – there is a qualitative difference that seems obvious to my eyes. Nevertheless, while continuously contributing my share to the political and intellectual struggle against Western imperialist policies, I feel it is my duty, as always, to criticise what I deem to be misleading views on the opposite side of the political divide, whatever convergence I may have with their holders on some crucial issues.

Notes

1   The June 1967 war accelerated the conversion of "objective Marxism" into "subjective Marxism" in the Arab world, as Abdallah Laroui had foreseen on the eve of the war. See his book *L'idéologie arabe contemporaine*, preface by Maxime Rodinson, Paris: François Maspero, 1967.

2   Sadik Jalal al-'Azm, "Orientalism and Orientalism in Reverse", in *Khamsin 8*, London: Ithaca Press, 1981 (the article is dated "Autumn 1980"), pp. 5–26. Reproduced in A. L. Macfie, ed., *Orientalism: A Reader*, New York: NYU Press, 2000, pp. 217–38.

3   Al-'Azm, *Al-istishraq wal-istishraq maakusan*, Beirut: Dar al-Hadatha, 1981.

4   *Khamsin*, p. 18; Macfie, ed., p. 230.

5   *Khamsin*, p. 22; Macfie, ed., p. 234.

6   See his 1978–79 articles and interviews on Iran collected in Michel Foucault, *Dits et écrits II, 1976–1988*, Paris: Gallimard, 2001, pp. 662–794. These texts were translated and published in English in the appendix of Janet Afary and Kevin B. Anderson, *Foucault and the Iranian Revolution: Gender and the Seductions of Islamism*, Chicago: University of Chicago Press, 2005, pp. 189–267.

7   Foucault's worst article was published in the French weekly magazine *Le Nouvel Observateur* in October 1978 under the title "What are the Iranians dreaming about?" (*Dits et écrits II*, pp. 688–94; Afary and Anderson, pp. 203–9). On Foucault's "divagations" about Iran, see the bitter and vigorous comment by Maxime Rodinson in his *L'Islam: politique et croyance*, Paris: Fayard, 1993, pp. 301–27; and the English translation in the appendix to *Foucault and the Iranian Revolution*, pp. 267–77.

8   Guy Hocquenghem, *Lettre ouverte à ceux qui sont passés du col Mao au Rotary* (1986), Marseille: Agone, 2003, preface by Serge Halimi.

9   Olivier Roy, "Les islamologues ont-ils inventé l'islamisme?", *Esprit*, August-September 2001, pp. 116–36.

10   For an argumentation about the perfectly legitimate use of the term and concept of "fundamentalism", see al-'Azm's excellent essay "Islamic Fundamentalism Reconsidered: A Critical Outline of Problems, Ideas and Approaches", Parts I and II, in *South Asia Bulletin*, XIII 1&2, 1993, pp. 93–121, and XIV 1, 1994, pp. 73–98.

11   Expressions such as "political Islam" or "militant Islam" share the same flaw.

12   Jean-François Clément, 'Pour une compréhension des mouvements islamistes', *Esprit*, January 1980, pp. 38–51.

13   Olivier Carré, *La légitimation islamique des socialismes arabes. Analyse conceptuelle combinatoire des manuels scolaires égyptiens, syriens et irakiens*, Paris: FNSP, 1979. Carré's "hypothesis" is summed up on p. 257.

14   For a discussion of this matter, see my article, "Religion and Politics Today from a Marxian Perspective" [in this same collection].

15   Carré, "L'utopie islamiste au Moyen-Orient arabe et particulièrement en Egypte et en Syrie", co-authored with Michel Seurat (each one's contribution is distinguished from the other's) in Carré, ed., *L'Islam et l'Etat dans le monde d'aujourd'hui*, Paris: PUF, 1982, pp. 13–20 (Carré's section). Carré thus lent his scholarly authority to the

use of the term "Islamism", against which Maxime Rodinson had argued.

16   Carré and Gérard Michaud (a pseudonym used by Seurat), ed., *Les Frères musulmans Égypte et Syrie (1928–1982)*, Paris: Gallimard/Julliard, 1983.

17   Ibid., p. 205.

18   Ibid., p. 219.

19   Ibid., p. 218.

20   Ibid., p. 203.

21   Claire Brière, Olivier Carré, *Islam: Guerre à l'Occident?*, Paris: Autrement, 1983. Claire Brière, a French journalist, had previously co-authored a book on the Iranian Revolution that was regarded as overenthusiastic (Claire Brière and Pierre Blanchet, *Iran: La révolution au nom de Dieu*, Paris: Seuil, 1979). It included an interesting interview with Michel Foucault that contributed, however, to the latter's moment of disgrace when the new Iranian regime started displaying its authoritarian features (Foucault, *Dits et écrits II*, pp. 743–55).

22   Carré, "L'Islam politique en Égypte", in Brière and Carré, *Islam: Guerre à l'Occident?*, p. 138.

23   Ibid., p. 172.

24   Gilles Kepel, *Le Prophète et Pharaon. Les mouvements islamistes dans l'Egypte contemporaine*, Paris: La Découverte, 1984; English translation: *The Prophet and Pharaoh: Muslim Extremism in Contemporary Egypt*, London: Saqi, 1985.

25   Roy, *L'Afghanistan. Islam et modernité politique*, Paris: Seuil, 1985; English translation: *Islam and Resistance in Afghanistan*, Cambridge: Cambridge University Press, 1986.

26   *L'Afghanistan*, p. 11; *Islam and Resistance in Afghanistan*, pp. 2–3 (mistranslated).

27   *L'Afghanistan*, pp. 12–13; *Islam and Resistance in Afghanistan*, pp. 3–4.

28   *L'Afghanistan*, p. 17; *Islam and Resistance in Afghanistan*, p. 8.

29   *L'Afghanistan*, p. 94; *Islam and Resistance in Afghanistan*, p. 69.

30   *L'Afghanistan*, p. 110; *Islam and Resistance in Afghanistan*, pp. 82–3 (translation revised).

31   *L'Afghanistan*, p. 214; *Islam and Resistance in Afghanistan*, p. 156 (translation revised).

32   François Burgat, *L'islamisme au Maghreb: La voix du Sud*, Paris: Karthala, 1988. An English updated edition was published four years later: *The Islamic Movement in North Africa*, Austin: University of Texas, 1992. The book was translated by William Dowell, then correspondent of *Time* magazine in Cairo, and bore his name as co-author, probably because he brought important changes to the original edition; there are many differences between the two versions. This is why I have preferred to select quotes from the French edition and translate them directly myself – references are to the third French edition of Burgat's book: *L'islamisme au Maghreb*, Paris: Payot, 1995.

33   Burgat, "De la difficulté de nommer: intégrisme, fondamentalisme, islamisme", *Les Temps modernes*, March 1988, p. 137.

34   Burgat, *L'islamisme au Maghreb*, p. 80.

35   Ibid., p. 68.

36   Ibid., p. 70.

37   Ibid., pp. 71–2.

38 Tehran at the time was engaged in an "asymmetric campaign" (to use military jargon) against France in retaliation for the heavy involvement of Paris on Baghdad's side in the Iraq–Iran War.

39 Carré, *L'Utopie islamique dans l'Orient arabe*, Paris: FNSP, 1991, p. 16. The term "barbarism" was applied by Seurat to the Syrian regime – see his article under the pseudonym Gérard Michaud, "L'État de barbarie, Syrie 1979–1982", *Esprit*, November 1983, reproduced in a posthumous collection bearing the same title, Seurat, *L'État de barbarie*, Paris: Seuil, 1989.

40 Farhad Khosrokhavar, "Du néo-orientalisme de Badie: enjeux et méthodes", *Peuples méditerranéens*, 50, January–March 1990. This is a brilliant polemical essay against Bertrand Badie.

41 Gilbert Achcar, *The Clash of Barbarisms*, 2nd augmented ed., London: Saqi Books, p. 167, n. 33.

42 *L'Utopie islamique*, p. 16.

43 Carré, *L'Islam laïque ou le retour à la Grande Tradition*, Paris: Armand Colin, 1993.

44 Ibid., p. 136.

45 Roy, *L'Échec de l'Islam politique*, Paris: Seuil, 1992; English edition: *The Failure of Political Islam*, Cambridge, MA: Harvard University Press, 1994.

46 *L'Échec de l'Islam politique*, p. 39; *The Failure of Political Islam*, p. 23 (translation revised).

47 *L'Échec de l'Islam politique*, p. 102; *The Failure of Political Islam*, p. 75.

48 *L'Échec de l'Islam politique*, p. 10; *The Failure of Political Islam*, pp. ix–x.

49 Roy, *L'islam mondialisé*, Paris: Seuil, 2002.

50 Roy, *Globalised Islam: The Search for a New Ummah*, London: Hurst & Co., 2004.

51 Ibid., pp. 3–4.

52 Ibid., p. 64.

53 Ibid., pp. 1–2.

54 Ibid., p. 88.

55 Ibid., p. 1.

56 Ibid., p. 97.

57 Ibid., p. 52.

58 Ibid., p. 307.

59 Ibid., p. 48.

60 Roy, "Why Do They Hate Us? Not Because of Iraq", *New York Times*, 22 July 2005.

61 Roy, "L'Iran fait monter les enchères", *Le Monde*, 21 July 2006.

62 Roy, "We're winning, despite the 'war'", *International Herald Tribune*, 7 September 2006.

63 Burgat, *L'islamisme en face*, Paris: La Découverte, 1995; English translation: *Face to Face with Political Islam*, London: I. B. Tauris, 2003. *L'islamisme à l'heure d'Al-Qaida*, Paris: La Découverte, 2005.

64 *L'islamisme en face*, p. 100; *Face to Face with Political Islam*, p. 65.

65 Al-'Azm, "Orientalism and Orientalism in Reverse", *Khamsin*, p. 25; Macfie, ed., p. 237.

66 Maxime Rodinson, *La fascination de l'Islam*, Paris: Maspero, 1980, p. 100; English translation: *Europe and the Mystique of Islam*, London: I. B. Tauris, 1988, pp. 76–7 (translation revised).

Marx, Engels and "Orientalism": On Marx's Epistemological Evolution

There can hardly be any doubt that Edward Said's 1978 *Orientalism* "has had a place in the long and often interrupted road to human freedom", as Said himself pleaded at the end of the "Preface to the Twenty-Fifth Anniversary Edition" of his most famous book.[1] He wrote that Preface in May 2003, barely four months before his demise, and it can be regarded as his testament in this respect. *Orientalism* has in fact been a prominent landmark on that long road to freedom, and will undoubtedly remain acknowledged as such by future generations.

Said's *Orientalism* and its Marxist critique

If Said's book played such an important role, it was certainly not because it was an uncontroversial piece of scholarship. Quite the contrary: it is the huge controversy that *Orientalism* provoked that made it such an outstanding milestone in the history of ideas. The book proved a watershed in the exposure, on a mass scale, of a pervasive and deeply entrenched "Western" Eurocentric colonial mindset; it forced academia into an epistemological break of a magnitude equating to a paradigm shift.

Orientalism's central and most important thesis – the critique of that mindset's essentialist view of the Orient, which Said endeavoured to deconstruct in some of its major manifestations – was not original, though. One can find a quite comprehensive statement of the fundamentals of this critique in Anouar Abdel-Malek's article "Orientalism in Crisis", published in 1963 in the English edition of the international journal of social sciences *Diogenes*.[2] Said duly acknowledged his debt to Abdel-Malek, quoting his article extensively and repeatedly in his own book. Likewise, in 1968 Maxime Rodinson wrote a remarkable critique of Eurocentrism at work in "The Western Image and Western Studies of Islam", of which an abridged version was published in English translation in 1974.[3] Said, in turn, heaped praise on Rodinson in his own seminal book, quoting the 1968/1974 piece as well as Rodinson's *Islam and Capitalism*.[4] All in all, Said's *Orientalism* is one instance of many whereby a talented author has given a much wider resonance to a thesis already formulated by others, by restating it in a more straightforward and thus more provocative manner, and elaborating upon it.

If *Orientalism* provoked such a vast controversy, it was not only due to the reaction of those who were targeted in the book and the barons of the field that Said devastated. The book was also criticised by thinkers sharing with Said the anti-colonial/anti-imperialist standpoint. The fact is that the book was not flawless. For all Said's talent he could not hide the limits of his familiarity with the vast field of Oriental Studies, in which he was no specialist. Nor could he avoid some of the methodological pitfalls that lie in wait for anyone who embarks on demolishing a system of thought in the absence of an alternative perspective that is more than a spontaneous counter-system reproducing, upside-down, many of the same flaws that mar the original.[5]

The most balanced and perceptive early assessment of Said's

book from a standpoint sharing its anti-colonial premises was made by none other than Rodinson, in the introduction to the 1980 original French edition of his *Europe and the Mystique of Islam*.[6] There, Rodinson emphasised Said's "merit" in contributing to the exposure of the ideology of British and French Orientalism in colonial and postcolonial times, describing his analysis as "intelligent, sagacious, and often pertinent" and stressing the validity of many of Said's criticisms of traditional Orientalism. He rightly asserted that

> the shock effect of [Said's] book will prove very useful if it leads the specialists to understand that they are not as innocent as they say, or even as they believe, to try to detect the general ideas from which they unconsciously derive their inspiration, to become conscious of these ideas, and to submit them to critical inspection.[7]

Yet Rodinson's commendation went along with a far-sighted warning on the danger inherent in some of Said's analyses and formulations. He asserted that, "stretched to the limit and pushed to the extreme" (as they would be by many of Said's self-proclaimed disciples, though Rodinson, writing in 1980, was only using the conditional tense), these could lead to the development of a dogmatic doctrine that dismissed, *a priori*, any findings labelled "Orientalist" in the name of an "anti-Orientalist" outlook – in a manner reminiscent of the Stalinist tradition (the Zhdanov Doctrine).[8] "Postcolonial" rather than "anti-Orientalist" is the label that was to be used and misused later on in this regard. Regrettably, Said reacted with invectives, shifting from the admiration of Rodinson that he expressed in *Orientalism* to, at times rather base, public attacks.[9]

However, despite his unbecoming lack of tolerance of criticism,

Said heeded Rodinson's warning, which he appropriated in his 1985 "Orientalism Reconsidered" (while treating Rodinson with scorn in the same essay). There he warned of exactly the same problem to which Rodinson had pointed, the problem of

> whether in identifying and working through anti-dominant critiques, subaltern groups – women, blacks, and so on – can resolve the dilemma of autonomous fields of experience and knowledge that are created as a consequence. A double kind of possessive exclusivism could set in: the sense of being an excluding insider by virtue of experience (only women can write for and about women, and only literature that treats women or Orientals well is good literature), and second, being an excluding insider by virtue of method (only Marxists, anti-Orientalists, feminists can write about economics, Orientalism, women's literature).[10]

The one set of critics with whom Said never really engaged consisted of those Marxists of the Orient (Arabs, South Asians) who, like Rodinson, shared Said's anticolonial and anti-imperialist standpoint, but who exposed important flaws in his critique of Orientalism and criticised him for what they perceived as his misinterpretation of Marx. They were particularly irritated by Said's indiscriminate classification of Marx as an "Orientalist" in the pejorative sense, in full disregard of the fact that most anticolonial and anti-imperialist struggles in the twentieth century were inspired by Marx's legacy.

Said's summary repudiation of Marx was all the less legitimate in that many of the direct inspirations of his critique of Orientalism regarded Marx as their principal methodological reference. The author of *Orientalism* could therefore be rightly accused of "theoretical eclecticism" by Aijaz Ahmad, who protested against

the way in which "sweeping, patently poststructuralist denuncia-
tions of Marxism can be delivered in the name of Gramsci, using
the terminology explicitly drawn from Althusser, and listing the
names of communist poets like Aimé Césaire, Pablo Neruda and
Mahmoud Darwish to illustrate the sites of resistance".[11]

The fact is that Said never engaged seriously with Marxism, nor
with his Marxist critics for that matter. His ambivalence towards
Marxism appeared to be at least partly the result of a contradiction
between, on one hand, his own support for all aspects of human
emancipation, and on the other, his professional location at the
very centre of US academia – in the academic "belly of the beast"
– where Marxism was anathema, especially in the intensifying
Cold War years during which Said rose to prominence. Said's
commitment to human emancipation – to "human, and
humanistic, desire or enlightenment and emancipation", as he
himself put it in his 2003 preface to *Orientalism* – led to the fact
that "much that was best in his work was, in the end, at one with
the best parts of the Marxist intellectual tradition", as Stephen
Howe concluded in a remarkable discussion of Said's relation
to Marxism.[12] The aforementioned contradiction provides a
sociological clue to those "anxieties of [Marxist] influence" that
Howe detected in Said's stance, although he overlooked their
social underpinning, i.e. what constitutes indeed the primary
locus of political conscience in Marxist understanding.

In any event, Said felt much more at ease replying to hawkish
pro-imperialist intellectuals like Bernard Lewis, Fouad Ajami, or
Kanan Makiya, than engaging with the likes of Sadik Jalal al-
'Azm, Mahdi 'Amil, Samir Amin, or Aijaz Ahmad.[13] In his 1994
"Afterword" to *Orientalism*, he contented himself with a very
offhand allusion to "dogmatic critics in the Arab world and
India" who maintain – so Said claimed – that Marx's thought has
"risen above his obvious prejudices".[14] Lacking a direct experience

of Arab politics other than dealing with the upper crust of the Palestine Liberation Organisation (PLO) for which he acted for several years as a quasi-diplomatic representative in the US, Said failed to understand the reason for the Oriental Marxists' anger with him.

Orientalism, essentialism and idealism

The reason for their anger was primarily the congruence between Said's tenuous characterisation of Marxism as "Orientalist" and the traditional endeavour by the upholders of ethnocentric views in the Orient – whether ultra-nationalists or religious fundamentalists – to disqualify the Marxists from the struggle against Western domination under the pretence that Marxism is a "Western" import and that Marx's followers are therefore unfit for duty. It is the reason why the Lebanese Communist Mahdi 'Amil reproached Said so bitterly and forcefully for having himself adhered to the essentialist mindset that he debunked in "Western" perceptions of the Orient, to the point of playing to the tune of the nationalists and traditionalists. 'Amil's vigorous Althusserian critique of Said's *Orientalism* was published in 1985. In a tragic illustration of the issue that provoked his ire, 'Amil was assassinated two years later by Shi'i Islamic fundamentalists who wanted to deny him and his party, within the Lebanese Shi'i community to which he belonged by birth,[15] the legitimacy of armed resistance to the Israeli occupation of Lebanon that the Communists initiated in 1982.

'Amil branded Said's critique of Western thinking as itself falling into the trap of essentialism, in that it lumped Marx together with other "Western" thinkers on the basis of a geographical definition of their cultural location. This was in full disregard of the social epistemological fault line that Marx instituted: his radical criticism from a working-class perspective of the entire body of bourgeois thinking. For this reason, 'Amil characterised Said's own thought as "idealist" in the philosophical meaning of the term, methodological idealism being – by definition – the matrix of essentialism in all its manifestations.

As a matter of fact, the main weakness in Said's *Orientalism* stems from its author's lack of familiarity with philosophy. One result of this deficiency is that Said dealt mostly with manifestations of the "Orientalist" mindset in the fields of linguistics and literature, the latter being the most familiar to him, and very little with that mindset's instances in the fields of philosophy and social sciences. Yet such instances are more determining, if only because their influence on politics is more direct than that of literature, let alone linguistics.

Thus, despite his immeasurable influence, Max Weber is only discussed once and briefly in Said's book and from what is obviously a second-hand acquaintance based on Maxime Rodinson's discussion of Weber in his *Islam and Capitalism*. Moreover, aside from this passing reference to Weber and the summary repudiation of Marx as "Orientalist", there is hardly any discussion in Said's book of the vast corpus of Western philosophy and social theory. A crucial correlate of this shortcoming is that Said overlooks the fact that "Orientalism" as an essentialism is deeply rooted in philosophical/methodological idealism, as it believes that the fate of peoples is determined by their perennial culture, their religion above all. In his 1968 text "Western Views of the Muslim World", Rodinson had explained the rationale behind the development of this perspective in the nineteenth century:

> The history of religions grew out of the struggle between bourgeois relativist pluralism and the ideological monopoly of

Christianity. It stimulated great interest in the study of Eastern religions as alternatives to Christianity both in the past and in the present. As part of the era's underlying theoretical idealism, the new historians of religion inculcated the idea that the essence of each civilization is spiritual: religion permeates and explains every aspect of civilization.[16]

The fact that Said expressed only (albeit brilliantly) what was already very much in the spirit of the times is strikingly illustrated by the publication in 1978 – the same year as Said's best-selling book – of another radical critique of Orientalism from a Marxist standpoint, that of Bryan Turner in his *Marx and the End of Orientalism*.[17] It also shows the epistemological superiority of the Marxist critique of Orientalism over Said's, which failed to criticise historical idealism as the main matrix of cultural essentialism. Turner's description of Orientalism is much less famous than Said's despite its being more complex and more complete than the latter – or perhaps, precisely because it is so. Limiting his discussion to Orientalism as applied to Islam in the Middle East and North Africa, Turner defined its roots as follows:

> Orientalism is based on an epistemology which is essentialist, empiricist and historicist. The essentialist assumption is present in the notion that "Islam" is a coherent, homogeneous, global entity, and also in the decline thesis where Islam is seen as declining because of some flaw in its essence. ... This inner, flawed essence unfolds in history as a teleological process toward some final end-state which is the collapse of Islam and its civilisation. In this historicist approach, the dynamic history of Western civilisation, punctured by constant, progressive revolutions, is contrasted with the static history of Islam in which popular uprisings are merely an index of

despotism and decay. ...

The teleology of historical progress and the East-West contrast in both forms of historicism have their origin in Hegel's attempt to come to terms with the problem of Christianity in a society with an increasing division of labour.[18]

Overlooking the connection between essentialism and philosophical idealism, Said does not mention even once in *Orientalism* what is certainly the most characteristic statement of the Western "Orientalist" outlook – which, unsurprisingly, is to be found in the apex of idealist philosophy that Hegel embodied. In contrast, Turner's location of the origin of modern Orientalism in Hegelian philosophy is very true and crucial. Indeed, Hegel's depiction of the "Oriental World" in the *Lectures on the Philosophy of World History* that he taught in 1821–31 is at once the most glaring and most sophisticated synopsis of "Orientalist" clichés that has ever been written.[19] In it, Islam is construed as the antithesis of the "Germanic World", which constitutes in Hegel's typical ethnocentric assessment "the Spirit of the new World".

The perception of Islam that prevails to this day in "Orientalist" thinking oscillates between two poles that are most concisely expounded in Hegel's description of "Mahometanism". On one hand, explains Hegel, Muslims ("Mahometans") were initially characterised by

... *Fanaticism*, that is, an enthusiasm for something abstract – for an abstract thought which sustains a negative position towards the established order of things. It is the essence of fanaticism to bear only a desolating destructive relation to the concrete; but that of Mahometanism was, at the same time, capable of the greatest elevation – an elevation free from all petty interests, and united with all the virtues that appertain to magnanimity and valor. *La religion et la terreur* were the principles in this case, as with Robespierre *la liberté et la terreur.*[20]

This "fanaticism" enabled the Muslims to achieve great deeds, greater than those that any other "fanaticism" ever achieved. However, explains Hegel, on the basis of such "enthusiasm for something abstract", nothing is solid. Thus the great Arabian empire did not last long.

> Fanaticism having cooled down, no moral principle remained in men's souls. ... [T]he East itself, when by degrees enthusiasm had vanished, sank into the grossest vice. The most hideous passions became dominant, and as sensual enjoyment was sanctioned in the first form which Mahometan doctrine assumed, and was exhibited as a reward of the faithful in Paradise, it took the place of fanaticism. At present, driven back into its Asiatic and African quarters, and tolerated only in one corner of Europe through the jealousy of Christian Powers, Islam has long vanished from the stage of history at large, and has retreated into Oriental ease and repose.[21]

At its most deeply rooted core, the "Orientalist" reading of our contemporary history has it that Islam eventually came out of this sensual apathy only to sink into a purely negative version of its initial fanaticism of "religion and terror", Islam being eternally caught between these two constitutive poles of its doctrine in Hegel's interpretation. Thus, as in all idealist interpretations of history, historical phenomena are fundamentally explained as cultural outcomes, as the results of the ideology upheld by their actors, in full disregard of the vast array of social, economic and political circumstances that led to the emergence and prevalence of this or that version of an ideology among particular social groups.

Marx and Engels' radical break
with historical idealism

Any student of Marx knows that the interpretation of history he developed is based on the most radical rejection of philosophical idealism ever to emerge in the study of society. Indeed, the first stage in the genesis of Marx's original thought was entirely devoted to the critique of the idealist philosophy of Hegel and his epigones. A major moment in this first stage was devoted to a criticism of the idealist critique of religion as formulated by the Young Hegelians, especially Ludwig Feuerbach and Bruno Bauer.

The first articulation of Marx's break with the idealist interpretation of history to be published in his own time dealt with the explanation of history by religion. This was his 1843 critique of two essays by Bauer: *The Jewish Question* and another on Jews and Christians. However, in that famous twofold rebuttal entitled *On the Jewish Question*, Marx had not yet completely broken with an essentialist appraisal of religion – Judaism and Christianity in that case – in the vein of Feuerbach's half-baked materialist critique of the Christian religion, characteristically entitled *The Essence of Christianity*.[22]

Thus, while inverting the postulated relation between religion and society in a materialist direction, Marx was still dealing with a basically essentialist perception of religion, discussing the "essence" of Judaism and Christianity in idealisations called "the Jew" and "the Christian". The singular in such expressions bears witness to the persistence of methodological idealism. The essence of "the Jew" and "Judaism" in Marx's anti-Bauer essays is defined by monetary relations. Marx contends that this essence is the result not of the Jewish religion *per se*, but of the actual historical insertion of Jews "in the pores" or "in the interstices" of medieval [European] societies, as he put it much later in his economic manuscripts.[23]

Bauer considers that the *ideal*, abstract nature of the Jew, his *religion*, is his *entire* nature. ... Let us consider the actual, worldly Jew – not the *Sabbath Jew*, as Bauer does, but the *everyday Jew*. Let us not look for the secret of the Jew in his religion, but let us look for the secret of his religion in the real Jew. ...

The Jew has emancipated himself in a Jewish manner, not only because he has acquired financial power, but also because, through him and also apart from him, *money* has become a world power and the practical Jewish spirit has become the practical spirit of the Christian nations. The Jews have emancipated themselves insofar as the Christians have become Jews. ... Judaism continues to exist not in spite of history, but owing to history. ... The god of the Jews has become secularized and has become the god of the world.[24]

The persistence of the essentialist perspective clearly manifests itself in Marx's reiteration of this criticism of Bauer in the first book he co-authored with Friedrich Engels, *The Holy Family*:

Herr Bauer grasps *only the religious* essence of Jewry, but not the *secular, real basis* of that religious essence. He combats *religious consciousness* as if it were something independent. Herr Bauer therefore explains the *real* Jews by the *Jewish religion*, instead of explaining the mystery of the Jewish religion by the *real Jews*.[25]

In these early writings by Marx, the materialist overturn of the idealist perspective consists in turning upside down the postulated relationship between the "essence" and the "real basis". However, the materialist perspective is still incomplete in that the very concept of "essence" remains unchallenged. Marx's radical break with essentialism, i.e. the true completion of his break with methodological idealism, will occur with the inception of his and Engels' historical materialist outlook. This is the moment Louis Althusser called the "epistemological break" in Marx's intellectual evolution, borrowing a concept elaborated by Gaston Bachelard.[26]

It is in Marx and Engels' joint 1845–46 manuscript *The German Ideology* (unpublished during their lifetime) that the gestation of their groundbreaking interpretation of history took place. It is there indeed that we read the first clear repudiation of essentialism *per se* under their pen, with a radical criticism of the notion of "essence" while the term itself is used most of the time between quotation marks: "This sum of productive forces, capital funds and social forms of intercourse, which every individual and every generation finds in existence as something given, is the real basis of what the philosophers have conceived as 'substance' and 'essence of man' ...".[27] To the idealist generic view of the Human as an essence, Marx and Engels substituted the existence of real human beings who evolve in the course of history. Hence they identify Feuerbach's fundamental flaw in that "he says 'the Humans' instead of the 'real historical humans'".[28]

It must already be clear at this point that, whatever characterisation of Oriental countries one may find in Marx's view (we shall examine this in the following pages), the epistemological revolution that he and Engels initiated is the most radical repudiation of all brands of essentialism – in fact, the *only* radical repudiation of essentialism. If Orientalism in the pejorative sense consists of adhering to a set of prejudices about the Oriental (Muslim, Arab, Indian, etc.) "cultural nature", there is no more radical rejection of this perspective than a conception that discounts the very idea of a "cultural nature" in order to explain *every* cultural form as the historical product of the material circumstances shaping the existence of the human group that bears the culture in question

– a culture that will inevitably be altered when the material circumstances themselves change.

This crucial premise is the key to two consequences of Said's poor knowledge of Marx: first, while he put Marx squarely in the same bag as the Orientalists he targeted in his book,[29] Said failed to reflect upon the conspicuous fact that the two most direct inspirations for his critique of the skewed representation of the Orient pervasive in the West – namely, Abdel-Malek and Rodinson – were both Marxists. The core theses of *Orientalism* that are most immune to criticism, i.e. those that Said borrowed from both thinkers, are deeply rooted in the Marxist fundamentals common to them beyond their differences. The theoretically soundest and most powerful characterisation of flawed Orientalism in Said's book is actually the long one-page excerpt of Abdel-Malek's 1964 article that he quoted and partly misquoted.[30] There can be no denying that the criticism of essentialism as the key methodological flaw of mainstream Orientalism, which is common to both Abdel-Malek and Rodinson, stems directly from their common adherence to the Marxist materialist interpretation of history and its criticism of historical idealism. Said, however, seemed to be totally oblivious to this fact.

The other consequence of Said's unfamiliarity with Marx – especially his lack of awareness of the fact that criticism of historical idealism is the cornerstone of any criticism of essentialism – is that, unlike Abdel-Malek and Rodinson, he could not transcend the essentialism he criticised. Thus his critique of Western essentialist views of the Orient is itself essentialist at its core, premised as it is upon an essentialist definition of the West. This was underlined by Said's Oriental Marxist critics – al-'Azm, 'Amil, Amin and Ahmad – who all reproached him for adhering to a construction of the West that postulates a continuity from Ancient Greece to the present US, and for positing that true knowledge of the Orient is beyond the reach of Western minds, thus pandering to Oriental ethnocentrisms and their own mythical representation of their communities (what al-'Azm called "Orientalism in reverse").

Were Marx and Engels Eurocentric?

The question that is therefore warranted, *a priori*, is not whether or not Marx is "Orientalist" in the sense of adhering to an essentialist, culturalist view of the "Orient"; he definitely did not adhere to such a perspective from the moment he completed his break with historical idealism. Nowhere in Marx's writings (except perhaps in private quips) will one encounter, thereafter, any depiction of "the Oriental", any Oriental people, or any people at all for that matter, as embodying an "essence" rooted in a perennial culture. This would have run directly counter to the key theoretical underpinning of Marx's view of the world and of history.

The question that is warranted is rather whether or not Marx is Eurocentric.[31] For however deep one's materialist rejection of essentialism, it does not suffice to create immunity against the danger of succumbing to ethnocentrism, which can very well dress in materialist garb. Despite the fact that the same writers who accuse Marx of Eurocentrism often accuse him likewise of "Orientalism", the two perspectives are not one and the same methodologically.[32] They must be separated if the discussion is to satisfy the requirements of intellectual rigour.

In fact, the concept of Eurocentrism itself ought to be split into two distinct types. One may be designated as *epistemic*, i.e. a Eurocentric perspective that results from insurmountable epistemological limitations such as those that faced a nineteenth-century observer without any direct experience of non-European societies. The other is *supremacist*, a type of Eurocentrism that is but a specific brand of ethnocentrism rooted in the global supremacy achieved by Western Europe starting from the nineteenth century.

That Marx's analyses of non-European societies were "epistemologically Eurocentric" is hardly disputable. From the historical materialist perspective he founded, it is acceptable to believe that he and Engels rose above their class of origin in adopting the standpoint of the working class, all the more so in that they built close ties with the workers' movement of their time. Yet it would be futile – or the unmistakable sign of a religious-like cult – to pretend that they could rise above the objective limitations in the study of non-European societies that resulted from the fact that their sources were all European and their knowledge of these societies only second-hand. Hence Marx and Engels – human, all too human as they were – were hostages to these limitations of their epoch, delving into the flawed European knowledge of non-European societies that was the only one available to them, as best illustrated by the now obvious flaws in their assessment of Indian history.[33]

In his remarkable discussion of this record, Daniel Thorner has very well shown how Marx and Engels' views were shaped to a great extent by what we may call the *episteme* of their time, using here the concept that was elaborated by Foucault in a book that came out in the same year (1966) that saw the publication of Thorner's article.[34] The earlier Marx and Engels were in their intellectual itinerary, the more compelling their epistemological limitations. The completion of their break with methodological idealism was not sufficient to free them entirely of the constraints of the existing episteme. Thorner has shown how their views on India in the late 1840s and early 1850s, including Marx's famous 1853 articles published in the *New York Daily Tribune*, were actually echoing – albeit in reverse causality – some of the deeply erroneous and prejudiced statements on India that Hegel expressed in his lectures on the *Philosophy of History*, India's purported historical stagnation in particular.

Marx's epistemic Eurocentrism manifested itself likewise in the belief that the European path of development would be followed by the rest of the world. European colonialism was therefore seen as fulfilling a historically progressive role in liberating the peoples of the "uncivilised" world (not the Orient alone, but what we would nowadays call the Global South) from their archaic shackles and putting them on the track of modernisation opened up by Europe.

This teleological conception of history – history as an ineluctable civilising process – is a direct legacy of the Enlightenment, and was very much part of the Zeitgeist of the mid-nineteenth century. It is combined with an important dose of positivism, albeit one that is more sophisticated than Auguste Comte's doctrine. Consequently, it is deeply anti-Romantic, holding nothing but scorn for all pre-capitalist pre-industrial social forms, whether European or non-European. To construe this, however, as Eurocentrism of the supremacist, ethnocentric type, of the type that led Hegel to assert that the "Germanic World" is "the Spirit of the new World", is to commit a serious misinterpretation.

Marx and Engels' early admiration is not for "their nation" but for a class – the bourgeoisie. Although recognising it as "the enemy" ever since they adhered as young men to the communist principle, they nonetheless praise its actions out of a belief in historical progress of a kind that leads inexorably to the communist end of history, progress of which the bourgeoisie is the "unconscious tool". This materialist–communist version of the Hegelian conception of History is laid down in the most naïve form in *The Communist Manifesto*, which sings the praises of the bourgeoisie:

The bourgeoisie, wherever it has got the upper hand, has put an end to all feudal, patriarchal, idyllic relations. ... It has drowned the most heavenly ecstasies of religious fervour, of chivalrous enthusiasm, of philistine sentimentalism, in the icy water of egotistical calculation. ...

The bourgeoisie has disclosed how it came to pass that the brutal display of vigour in the Middle Ages, which [reactionaries] so much admire, found its fitting complement in the most slothful indolence. It has been the first to show what man's activity can bring about. It has accomplished wonders far surpassing Egyptian pyramids, Roman aqueducts, and Gothic cathedrals ...

The bourgeoisie, by the rapid improvement of all instruments of production, by the immensely facilitated means of communication, draws all, even the most barbarian, nations into civilisation. ... It compels all nations, on pain of extinction, to adopt the bourgeois mode of production; it compels them to introduce what it calls civilisation into their midst, i.e., to become bourgeois themselves. In one word, it creates a world after its own image.

The bourgeoisie has subjected the country to the rule of the towns. It has created enormous cities, has greatly increased the urban population as compared with the rural, and has thus rescued a considerable part of the population from the idiocy of rural life. Just as it has made the country dependent on the towns, so it has made barbarian and semi-barbarian countries dependent on the civilised ones, nations of peasants on nations of bourgeois, the East on the West. ...

A similar movement is going on before our own eyes. ...

The weapons with which the bourgeoisie felled feudalism to the ground are now turned against the bourgeoisie itself.

But not only has the bourgeoisie forged the weapons that

bring death to itself; it has also called into existence the men
who are to wield those weapons – the modern working class –
the proletarians. …

What the bourgeoisie therefore produces, above all, is its
own grave-diggers. Its fall and the victory of the proletariat are
equally inevitable.[35]

As any reader of these famous lines from *The Communist Manifesto*
can tell, there is no Eurocentric contempt for non-Europeans at
work here, let alone "Orientalism", but a general contempt for all
pre-industrial forms of civilisation, European and non-European
alike. This grand historical narrative is as sarcastic towards the
legacy of feudal Europe and its "most slothful indolence", and
towards Europe's countryside and "the idiocy of rural life" as it
is towards "barbarian and semi-barbarian countries", "nations of
peasants", and "the East". All the achievements of past civilisations
are belittled, "Egyptian pyramids, Roman aqueducts, and Gothic
cathedrals" alike. This enthusiasm for the bourgeoisie as an
agent of historical change is of exactly the same kind as Hegel's
admiration for Napoleon, "this soul of the world", even though
the French emperor's troops were devastating the city where he
lived and taught.

It is this view that pervades Marx's 1853 statements on India,
and specifically the text quoted at length by Said in *Orientalism*.[36]
Although Marx expresses there, very briefly, some sorrow for the
Indian victims of British colonialism – whereas he had shown
only contempt for the peasants of the world, starting with those
of Europe, in *The Communist Manifesto* – the whole passage is
actually a critique of any Romantic temptation to idealise pre-
colonial India and its "idyllic village-communities", depicted in a
most negative manner. Like the world bourgeoisie forcing all societies out of agrarianism into industrialism, England is "causing

a social revolution" in India, albeit "actuated only by the vilest interests" and "stupid in her manner". "But that is not the question. The question is, can mankind fulfil its destiny without a fundamental revolution in the social state of Asia? If not, whatever may have been the crimes of England she was the unconscious tool of history in bringing about that revolution."[37]

At this point, Marx concluded his article with a quatrain from Goethe's *West–Eastern Divan*, which Said construes as "Romantic Orientalism" in a blatant misinterpretation, as the quatrain is an indirect reference to Napoleon, of whom Goethe was another great admirer. "Were not through the rule of Timur / Souls devoured without measure?" is believed to be an allusion to Napoleon's action in revolutionising German lands by subjugating them, and was certainly read as such by Marx. Far from being the expression of a "Romantic redemptive project" as Said puts it,[38] this is but a further acknowledgement of the progressive role of bourgeois violence in destroying ancient historical forms for which Marx's clear message is that no tears should be shed.[39]

It is exactly the same historical logic that is displayed in Engels' article on Algeria published in *The Northern Star* in 1848:

> [T]hough the manner in which brutal soldiers, like Bugeaud, have carried on the war is highly blameable, the conquest of Algeria is an important and fortunate fact for the progress of civilisation. ... And the conquest of Algeria has already forced the Beys of Tunis and Tripoli, and even the Emperor of Morocco, to enter upon the road of civilisation. They were obliged to find other employment for their people than piracy, and other means of filling their exchequer than tributes paid to them by the smaller states of Europe. And if we may regret that the liberty of the Bedouins of the desert has been destroyed, we must not forget that these same Bedouins were a nation of

robbers – whose principal means of living consisted of making excursions either upon each other, or upon the settled villagers, taking what they found, slaughtering all those who resisted, and selling the remaining prisoners as slaves. All these nations of free barbarians look very proud, noble and glorious at a distance, but only come near them and you will find that they, as well as the more civilised nations, are ruled by the lust of gain, and only employ ruder and more cruel means. And after all, the modern *bourgeois*, with civilisation, industry, order, and at least relative enlightenment following him, is preferable to the feudal lord or to the marauding robber, with the barbarian state of society to which they belong.[40]

The political/epistemological evolution of Marx and Engels

A major merit of Louis Althusser's reflection on the persistent Hegelianism detectable in Marx's writings until an advanced stage of his life is that it accustomed the students and disciples of Marx to the idea that the thinking of the author of *Das Kapital* did not spring up finished and flawlessly coherent from the time he "discovered" historical materialism. While applying Bachelard's concept of "epistemological break" to the development of Marx's thinking, Althusser identified a period of "maturation" in this thinking, i.e. an evolutionary process that followed the qualitative break with methodological idealism, and lasted, according to the author of *For Marx*, from 1845 until 1857, after which year Marx's thought reached its complete maturity and freedom from Hegelianism.

However, in pursuing his exploration of the Marxian corpus, Althusser found a more complex picture in the post-1857 writings, including *Das Kapital* itself – in which Marx flirted with Hegel's terminology, as he himself admitted. Althusser revised his assessment accordingly, indirectly acknowledging that Marx never rid himself completely of traces of Hegelian influence, except in very few writings in the last years of his life.[41] The truth is that Marx and Engels' thinking underwent a constant and gradual evolution in overcoming the epistemological constraints under which it had initially unfolded. This process could not be completed in their time, but only carried forward within limits set by the evolution of the epoch's episteme as determined by the build-up of knowledge.

It is no surprise that Hegel's intellectual influence on the two thinkers proved to be so lasting, as his impact on the history of thought has been so great that it is still very much felt in our own time. Indeed, Marx and Engels started to devise their own views by operating – very consciously – a materialist "inversion" of Hegel's dialectic. Marx characterised this in a rather un-dialectical way when he wrote that Hegel's dialectic is "standing on its head" and that turning it "right side up again" is all it takes to bring out its "rational kernel" from within the "mystical shell".[42] The logic of simple "inversion" is such that Marx and Engels remained under the influence of a Hegelian teleological perspective in their conception of history. It is only through the concurrence of several factors – political and epistemological – that they gradually shifted away from the Hegelian legacy towards a more consequent and complex materialist perspective. Yet, they did so without full awareness of their own evolution, and hence without radically completing their "epistemological break" with Hegel's influence. This is why traces of their initial inverted Hegelianism lingered in their writings until the end of their lives.

The error common to many critiques of Marx, Said's among them, as well as to many of Marx's self-proclaimed followers, is that they overlook the fact that his and Engels' thought was a body of work in the making throughout their lives and that it underwent a profound change over the years, starting from the time when they both settled in England in 1849. Colonialism and non-European societies were among the issues on which their thinking changed most, under the combined influence of new political experience and the general progress of knowledge. Thus, any comment on Marx's attitude towards India that considers his 1853 articles alone, without exploring the whole history of his statements on India until his last writings, and builds on those articles in order to formulate a general judgement on his "Orientalist" or "Eurocentric" bias, is fundamentally flawed and unsound.

Kevin Anderson published an exhaustive survey recently of the whole gamut of opinions and stances expressed by Marx over the years on national struggles, colonialism and non-European societies.[43] Like many other students of Marx before him, including the Indian Marxist historian Bipan Chandra,[44] he noted that Marx's stance on colonialism underwent a sharp radicalisation in the late 1850s.

> By 1856–57, the anticolonialist side of Marx's thought became more pronounced, as he supported, also in the *Tribune*, the Chinese resistance to the British during the Second Opium War and the Sepoy Uprising in India. During this period, he began to incorporate some of his new thinking about India into one of his greatest theoretical works, the *Grundrisse* (1857–58). In this germinal treatise on the critique of political economy, he launched into a truly multilinear theory of history, wherein Asian societies had developed along a different pathway than that of the successive modes of production he had delineated for Western Europe … While he had seen the Indian village's communal social forms as a prop of despotism in 1853, he

now stressed that these forms could be either democratic or despotic.[45]

One factor that contributed most to that result is undoubtedly Marx and Engels' discovery of the way in which English capitalist development was partly based on the plunder and de-development of Ireland, as Chandra rightly emphasised.[46] Here there was no equivalent of the objective Eurocentric epistemological constraints that marred their initial perception of non-European societies. Marx and Engels were in no way hostages to English ethnocentric representations of Anglo–Irish relations. They faced no language barrier in the access to Irish sources, nor did they lack direct access to Ireland itself, which Engels visited in 1856. Because they were not subjectively Eurocentric in the sense of ethnocentrism, their political sympathy for the Irish cause, in tune with that of the British workers' movement, led them to alter radically their perception of the impact of European colonialism on non-European societies as well. Ireland thus provided the key to India and Algeria.

The shift in Engels' assessment of Algeria between 1848 and 1857 could not be more radical. The "civilising role" of colonial capitalism towards "barbarian" countries vanished, to be replaced by a description of its rapacity and destructiveness:

From the first occupation of Algeria by the French to the present time, the unhappy country has been the arena of unceasing bloodshed, rapine, and violence. Each town, large and small, has been conquered in detail at an immense sacrifice of life. The Arab and Kabyle tribes, to whom independence is precious, and hatred of foreign domination a principle dearer than life itself, have been crushed and broken by the terrible razzias in which dwellings and property are burnt and destroyed, standing crops cut down, and the miserable wretches who remain massacred, or subjected to all the horrors of lust and brutality.[47]

This radical change in the perception of the role of European colonialism is reflected in the first volume of *Das Kapital* that Marx published in 1867. There colonialism is put where it belongs: as part of the gigantic rapacious plunder that was decisive in the constitution of capitalism by way of "primitive accumulation".

> The discovery of gold and silver in America, the extirpation, enslavement and entombment in mines of the aboriginal population, the beginning of the conquest and looting of the East Indies, the turning of Africa into a warren for the commercial hunting of black-skins, signalised the rosy dawn of the era of capitalist production. These idyllic proceedings are the chief momenta of primitive accumulation.[48]

Marx adds in this same section an ironic comment on the "Christian colonial system", quoting the Quaker William Howitt, whom he describes as "a man who makes a speciality of Christianity". Howitt's judgement is categorical and irrevocable: "The barbarities and desperate outrages of the so-called Christian race, throughout every region of the world, and upon every people they have been able to subdue, are not to be paralleled by those of any other race, however fierce, however untaught, and however reckless of mercy and of shame, in any age of the earth."[49] The final chapter of the first volume of *Das Kapital* is devoted to tearing to pieces the views of Edward Gibbon Wakefield, a prominent British advocate of colonisation and theorist of its purported "civilising mission".

One of the most regrettable consequences of the fact that

Marx did not write the volumes of *Das Kapital* on International-al Trade and on the World Market that he intended as the last instalments of the six-volume project described in his letter to Ferdinand Lassalle in 1858,[50] is that he did not develop the con-ception of a world capitalist system premised on the exploitation of a global periphery by an industrial capitalist core. There were intimations of this in his early writings, if overwhelmed by the Eurocentric teleological conception of historical progress that was still Marx's dominant perspective.[51] One can only share Chandra's regret that the author of *Das Kapital* did not develop an insight such as the one that appears in the first volume:

> By ruining handicraft production in other countries, machinery forcibly converts them into fields for the supply of its raw materials. In this way East India was compelled to produce cotton, wool, hemp, jute, and indigo for Great Britain. ... A new and international division of labour, a division suited to the requirements of the chief centres of modern industry springs up, and converts one part of the globe into a chiefly agricultural field of production, for supplying the other part which remains a chiefly industrial field.[52]

The corollary of Marx's break with his early Enlightenment-inspired teleological conception of history, is that he departed from the quasi-positivist anti-Romantic stance that went along with it. Instead of the scorn for pre-capitalist producers that he showed in his early years, the intense compassion for the victims of the capitalist "Moloch" displayed in *Das Kapital*, whether European peasants and artisans or non-European labourers and populations, is no longer heavily qualified to the point of being excused by heaping praise on the civilising role of the bourgeoisie and colonialism, the "unconscious tool of history".

In this respect, Marx was very much impressed and influenced in 1879 by the Russian anthropologist Maxim Kovalevsky's work on communal property in various lands, Mediterranean countries in particular – more than by his reading later on of Lewis Morgan's *Ancient Society*. As René Gallissot noted in 1976 in his excellent presentation of Marx's writings on Algeria, Marx remained, to be sure, objectively constrained by the limits of the knowledge of his time, but the epistemological evolution that he had accomplished in the last years of his life was considerable nevertheless.

> The end result is that Marx moved away, for sure, from his initial conception that he inherited from the Enlightenment and from the school of Hegelian philosophy, which saw history as running along a simple line from the Asiatic Orient to modern Western civilisation. His major achievement hitherto had been to elaborate a materialist version of the Hegelian historical process [*le devenir hégélien*], which evolved in the ether of ideas, if not of the fulfilment of the Idea, by basing the development of this process on the successive stages of production. Progressively, but more and more openly, Marx came to adopt a multilinear conception of history.[53]

Marx actually shifted to an increasingly "Romantic" vision of history, construing pre-capitalist collective forms of production that existed or had existed on the global periphery of Western Europe as forms that had the potential of combining with modern technology to provide relations of production that could be superior to those of capitalism. Copying out Kovalevsky's section on Algeria, he underlined how "the further maintenance of communal property", which was described in the debates at the French National Assembly in 1873 as "a form which supports communist tendencies in the mind", was seen by "the French bourgeois"

(Marx's comment) as "dangerous both for the colony and for the homeland".[54] In a remarkable shift from his long-standing view of the introduction of private property as a necessary stage in historical progress, Marx emphasised the observation that French colonialism's destruction of Algeria's communal property system did not even increase productivity overall.

> The introduction of private landownership among a population not prepared for it and antipathetic to it is to be the infallible panacea for the improvement of the means of agriculture, hence for the increase of productivity of the land. This [is] the cry not only of the Western European political economists, but even of the so-called "cultivated classes" of Eastern Europe! But not a single fact out of the history of colonization is brought forward ...[55]

The expropriation of the natives' communal property actually served only two goals: on the one hand, the appropriation of land by the colonists; on the other hand, "by tearing away the [natives] from their natural bond to the soil to break the last strength of the clan unions thus being dissolved, and thereby, any danger of rebellion."[56] Marx's verdict is categorical: "the light-bringing French" – as he describes them, sarcastically reproducing a quote found in Kovalevsky – committed "direct robbery!"[57] This is the background of the compassion for the natives and deep contempt for the European colonists that Marx expressed in his letters from Algeria, when visiting the country on his first and only trip out of Europe in 1882.

The late Marx's Romantic assessment of pre-capitalist communal property manifested itself most blatantly in his 1881 letter (and draft letters) to the Russian revolutionary Vera Zasulich in which, along with a remarkable statement of the idea

of uneven and combined development, he expressed his belief
that the Russian rural commune could mutate into a superior
form of collectivism depending on the historical surroundings.[58]
In this assessment, Marx came closer to the Romantic populism
of the Russian Narodniks than to what will be later regarded as
"orthodox Marxism" upheld against the Narodniks by the likes of
Georgi Plekhanov and Vladimir Lenin.

Critical Marxism and Orientalism

To sum up, the thought of Marx and Engels, assessed from the
very same historical materialist perspective for which they laid
the foundations, appears as an evolutionary critical endeavour to
overcome the epistemological constraints of their time – whether
those constraints were philosophical, principally represented by
Hegelian philosophy as the intellectual horizon of their epoch and
the main influence on their own thinking, or objective, inherent
in the limitations of the scholarship available to them. Thus the
corpus of Marx and Engels' work is itself ridden with the birth
pangs and contradictions intrinsic to a major intellectual watershed in the history of ideas, premised on a radical epistemological
break with the whole tradition of hitherto accumulated thinking.
Only the wildest brand of philosophical idealism could construe
this break as having been accomplished once and for all in a single moment instead of understanding that it could only unfold as
a protracted and progressive process.

The contradictions in Marx and Engels' thinking processes allowed for different views inspired by different parts or aspects of
their legacy. Thus, to be sure, there are positivist and teleological
brands of Marxism, some of them unmistakably Orientalist in
the pejorative sense, usually wrapping their essentialism in a radi-

cal stance towards religion and pre-modern cultures in general.[59] Nevertheless, the major breakthrough in the history of ideas that Marx and Engels developed provides the indispensable epistemological tool for a radical critique of all types of essentialism. This includes Orientalism, as Bryan Turner explained in 1978, in what reads now as an anticipatory critique of the limitations of Said's vigorous repudiation of "Orientalism":

> The criticism of Orientalism in its various forms requires something more than the valid but indecisive notion that at its worst Orientalist scholarship was a rather thin disguise for attitudes of moral or racial superiority ... and thereby a justification for colonialism. ... The end of Orientalism requires a fundamental attack on the theoretical and epistemological roots of Orientalist scholarship ... Modern Marxism is fully equipped to do this work of destruction, but in this very activity Marxism displays its own internal theoretical problems and uncovers those analytical cords which tie it to Hegelianism, to nineteenth-century political economy and to Weberian sociology.[60]

The great advantage of Marxian thought is that it is armed with a self-correcting methodology. This enables the student of Marxism to discern in the vast corpus of Marxism itself what is inconsistent with the ultimate logic of the materialist dialectical approach of history and society founded by Marx and Engels. As is obvious to anyone who is familiar with Marx's writings, his intellectual production is based above all on systematic *criticism*. Living Marxism is predicated upon the permanent exercise of this critical faculty, and the permanent critical and selective assimilation of advances achieved in all fields of human knowledge into the Marxist theory of history and society. Living Marxism is also and inseparably predicated upon the permanent exercise of self-criticism and self-correction in light of those advances.

In this sense, and whatever their shortcomings, the criticism of Marx in Said's *Orientalism* as well as the Said-inspired "postcolonial" criticisms of Marxism should be seen as welcome triggers of the self-critical and self-correcting faculty without which Marxism would have been truly and irrevocably dead for a very long time – instead of displaying the incomparable regenerating capability that bewilders all those who are only too eager to herald its death.

Notes

1   Edward Said, *Orientalism*, 25th Anniversary Edition with a New Preface by the Author, New York: Vintage Books, 2003, p. xxx.

2   Anouar Abdel-Malek, "Orientalism in Crisis", *Diogenes*, vol. 11, no. 44, 1963, pp. 103–40. An excerpt from this article can be found in Alexander Lyon Macfie, ed., *Orientalism: A Reader*, New York: NYU Press, 2000, pp. 47–56.

3   Maxime Rodinson, "The Western Image and Western Studies of Islam", in Joseph Schacht, ed. (posthumously) with C. E. Bosworth, *The Legacy of Islam*, Oxford: Clarendon Press, 1974; labelled as 2nd edn because Schacht had prepared a 1st edn before his death in 1969, pp. 9–62. The full text of Rodinson's original contribution in French was published in 1980, along with another illuminating text on Arab and Islamic Studies in Europe originally written in 1976, in *La fascination de l'Islam*, Paris: François Maspero, 1980, published in English as *Europe and the Mystique of Islam*, trans. Roger Veinus, Seattle: University of Washington Press, 1987.

4   Maxime Rodinson, *Islam and Capitalism*, trans. Brian Pearce, London: Allen Lane, 1974; repr. London: Saqi Books, 2007.

5   For a glimpse at the controversy provoked by Said's *Orientalism*, see the texts gathered in the above-quoted collection edited by A. L. Macfie, *Orientalism: A Reader*, and the survey of the debates by the same author in his own *Orientalism*, Harlow: Pearson Education, 2002.

6   Rodinson, *La fascination de l'Islam*, "Introduction", pp. 12-16.

7   Ibid., p. 14.

8   Ibid., pp. 14–15.

9   Said's worst attack came during an interview he gave in Paris in 1995, when, after describing Rodinson's remarks concerning his book as "totally scandalous", he added a comment that went beyond the pale of intellectual decency: "It does not

surprise me, coming from an ex-Stalinist, incapable as he is of understanding the nature of critique and more generally that of the critical method." Edward Said, *"Entretien avec Edward Said: Propos recueillis par Hassan Arfaoui et Subhi Hadidi"*, *M.A.R.S.*, no. 4, Winter 1995, p. 18. To be fair, however, only a few months earlier and in a publication by the same source (the Arab World Institute in Paris), Rodinson had given an *ad hominem* explanation of Said's *Orientalism*, attributing to the latter the frenetic zeal of a latecomer to a cause, who wants to make up for his sense of guilt after having kept aloof from the Palestinian cause during many years of academic advancement (Maxime Rodinson, *"Fantôme et réalités de l'orientalisme"*, *Qantara*, no. 13, Oct.–Dec. 1994, pp. 27–30).

10   Edward Said, "Orientalism Reconsidered", *Cultural Critique*, no. 1, Autumn 1985, p. 106.

11   Aijaz Ahmad, *In Theory: Classes, Nations, Literatures*, London: Verso, 1992, p. 200.

12   Stephen Howe, "Edward Said and Marxism: Anxieties of Influence", *Cultural Critique*, no. 67, Fall 2007, p. 81.

13   See Sadik Jalal al-'Azm, "Orientalism and Orientalism in Reverse", in *Khamsin 8*, London: Ithaca Press, 1981, pp. 5–26, rpt in Macfie, ed., *Orientalism: A Reader*, pp. 217–38; Mahdi 'Amil, *Hal al-qalb lil-sharq wal-'aql lil-gharb? Marx fi istishraq Edward Said*, Beirut: Al-Farabi, 1985; Samir Amin's brief discussion in his *Eurocentrism*, trans. R. Moore and J. Membrez, New York: Monthly Review Press, 1989; and, last but not least, Aijaz Ahmad's essay "*Orientalism* and After: Ambivalence and Metropolitan Location in the Work of Edward Said" (pp. 159– 219) in his above-quoted collection entitled *In Theory: Classes, Nations, Literatures*.

14   Said, *Orientalism*, pp. 338–9.

15   Mahdi 'Amil was of Shi'i descent, as was Hussein Mroué, another prominent Communist intellectual assassinated by the same murderers.

16   Rodinson, *Europe and the Mystique of Islam*, p. 61.

17   Bryan Turner, *Marx and the End of Orientalism*, London: George Allen & Unwin, 1978. In "Orientalism Reconsidered" (p. 102), Said heaped praise on Turner's book only to deface it as a criticism of Marxism in general instead of the committed *Marxist* critique of certain brands of Marxist thinking that it actually is. "Bryan Turner's exceptionally important little book", wrote Said, "went a very great part of the distance towards fragmenting, dissociating, dislocating, and decentering the experiential terrain covered at present by universalizing historicism; what he suggests in discussing the epistemological dilemma is the need to go beyond the polarities and binary oppositions of Marxist-historicist thought (voluntarisms vs. determinism, Asiatic vs. Western society, change vs. stasis) in order to create a new type of analysis of plural, as opposed to single, objects."

18   Ibid., pp. 7–8.

19   G. W. F. Hegel, *The Philosophy of History*, trans. J. Sibree, New York: Dover Publications, 1956.

20   Ibid., p. 358. On "fanaticism", see Alberto Toscano's *Fanaticism: On the Uses of an Idea*, London: Verso, 2010.

21   Hegel, *Philosophy of History*, p. 360.

22   See Louis Althusser's discussion of Feuerbach and his influence on the early Marx in the texts gathered in his *For Marx*, trans. Ben Brewster, Harmondsworth, UK:

Penguin, 1969.

23   Here are three statements shedding light on Marx's analysis of the economic role of Jews in history, from Karl Marx's *Grundrisse*, MECW, vols 28 and 29:
"Special trading peoples could play this mediating role between peoples whose mode of production did not yet presuppose exchange value as its basis. Thus in antiquity, and later the Lombards, thus the Jews within the old Polish society or in medieval society in general" (vol. 28, p. 184).
"Wealth as an end-in-itself appears only among a few trading peoples – monopolists of the carrying trade – who live in the pores of the ancient world like the Jews in medieval society" (vol. 28, p. 411).
"The less the whole internal economic structure of the society is still caught up by exchange value, the more they [participants in the exchange] appear as external extremes of circulation – firmly given in advance and taking a passive attitude to it. The whole movement as such appears independent with respect to them as intermediary trade whose carriers, such as the Semites in the interstices of the ancient world, and the Jews, Lombards and Normans in the interstices of the medieval society, alternately represent with respect to them the different moments of circulation – money and commodity. They are the mediators of the social exchange of matter" (vol. 29, p. 481).
This view was developed into a theory of the "people-class" by the young Marxist Abram Leon in the book he wrote in Nazi-occupied Belgium before being arrested and deported to Auschwitz, where he died in 1944 at the age of twenty-six: "*Above all the Jews constitute historically a social group with a specific economic function. They are a class, or more precisely, a people-class.*" *(The Jewish Question: A Marxist Interpretation,* available at the Marxists Internet Archive [www.marxists.org/subject/ jewish/leon/index.htm]; the quote is taken from Chapter One.) On Marxist discussions of "the Jewish question" from Marx to Leon, see Enzo Traverso, *The Marxists and the Jewish Question: The History of a Debate (1843–1943),* trans. Bernard Gibbons, Atlantic Highlands, NJ: Humanities Press, 1993.

24   Karl Marx, *On the Jewish Question*, MECW, vol. 3, pp. 169–72.

25   Karl Marx and Frederick Engels, *The Holy Family or Critique of Critical Criticism: Against Bruno Bauer and Company*, MECW, vol. 4, p. 109.

26   In Althusser's Preface of his *For Marx*.

27   Karl Marx and Frederick Engels, *The German Ideology*, MECW, vol. 5, p. 54 (emphasis added).

28   Ibid., p. 39. Translation corrected: the English translation wrongly uses the singular here ("he posits 'Man' instead of 'real historical [M]an'") whereas it is a plural in the original German text – "*er sagt 'den Menschen' statt d[ie] 'wirklichen historischen Menschen'*". This is a serious translation error, as the difference between "real historical [M]an" and "real historical men" is qualitative and crucial, the former phrase being an oxymoron in the final analysis.

29   Said's *Orientalism* is riddled with enumerations of nineteenth-century "Orientalists" that include Marx – "Writers as different as Marx, Disraeli, Burton, and Nerval" (p. 102), "every writer on the Orient, from Renan to Marx (ideologically speaking)" (p. 206), "such writers as Renan, Lane, Flaubert, Caussin de Perceval, Marx, and Lamartine" (p. 231) – and attributes to Marx most abusively a "homogenizing view

of the Third World" (p. 325), thus betraying a lack of familiarity with his work.

30   Ibid., p. 97. The misquoting is in the way Said, by means of ellipses and words between square brackets, abusively turned the two distinct groups that Abdel-Malek was assessing – traditional scholarly Orientalism on one hand and colonial agents of all sorts (academics, military men, missionaries, etc.), on the other – into one single group, thus blurring the distinctions that Abdel-Malek makes between them. Characteristically, Said deleted Abdel-Malek's description of the contribution of the first group as "multiple and fruitful". The worst distortion is when Abdel-Malek says that "both groups adopt an essentialist conception" while "the second group will soon proceed with it towards racism", whereas Said turns "both groups" into "[the Orientalists]" and replaces the reference to the second group with an ellipsis, so that "the Orientalists" all together become the ones who proceed towards racism.

31   For a recent good contribution to this discussion, see Kolja Lindner, "Marx's Eurocentrism: Postcolonial Studies and Marx Scholarship", *Radical Philosophy* 161 (May/June 2010), pp. 27–41.

32   Lindner's article fails to clearly draw this distinction, as it postulates from the beginning that "an 'Orientalist' way of looking at the non-Western world" is one dimension of the concept of Eurocentrism (ibid., p. 28). Likewise, one weakness of the above-quoted book by Bryan Turner is that it does not draw this qualitative distinction between Orientalism and Eurocentrism.

33   For an excellent critical appraisal of Marx's views on India and on colonialism from a Marxist perspective, see Bipan Chandra's "Karl Marx, His Theories of Asian Societies and Colonial Rule" in UNESCO, ed., *Sociological Theories: Race and Colonialism*, Paris: UNESCO, 1980, pp. 383–451. For a contextualisation of Marx's views on India, see Aijaz Ahmad, "Marx on India: A Clarification", in his *In Theory: Classes, Nations, Literatures*, pp. 221–42.

34   Daniel Thorner, "Marx on India and the Asiatic Mode of Production", *Contributions to Indian Sociology*, no. 9 (December 1966), pp. 33–66. Michel Foucault's book is, of course, *The Order of Things: An Archaeology of the Human Sciences*, London: Tavistock, 1970, the French original edition of which came out in 1966.

35   Karl Marx and Frederick Engels, *Manifesto of the Communist Party*, MECW, vol. 6, pp. 486–90, 496.

36   Said, *Orientalism*, pp. 153–4.

37   Karl Marx, "The British Rule in India", MECW, vol. 12, p. 132. Bill Warren tried to vindicate and update these flawed views of the immature Marx in his posthumously published *Imperialism: Pioneer of Capitalism*, John Senders, ed., London: Verso, 1980.

38   Said, *Orientalism*, p. 154.

39   On Romanticism, including a discussion of Marxism's relation to it, see Michael Löwy and Robert Sayre, *Romanticism Against the Tide of Modernity*, trans. Catherine Porter, Durham, NC: Duke University Press, 2001.

40   Frederick Engels, "Extraordinary Revelations. – Abd-El-Kader. – Guizot's Foreign Policy", MECW, vol. 6, pp. 471–2.

41   In Althusser's 1969 "Preface" to a French paperback edition of Marx's *Capital, Volume One*. The "Preface" was published in English translation in a collection

of his essays: Louis Althusser, *Lenin and Philosophy and Other Essays*, trans. Ben Brewster, London: New Left Books, 1971.

42   In Marx's 1873 "Afterword" to the second German edition of *Das Kapital*, MECW, vol. 35, p. 19. See Althusser's discussion of this statement in Louis Althusser and Etienne Balibar, *Reading Capital*, trans. Ben Brewster, London: New Left Books, 1970.

43   Kevin Anderson, *Marx at the Margins: On Nationalism, Ethnicity, and Non-Western Societies*, Chicago: University of Chicago Press, 2010.

44   Chandra, "Karl Marx, His Theories of Asian Societies and Colonial Rule". I myself came to the same conclusion (before reading Bipan Chandra) in a contribution on Marx and Engels' attitude towards war: Gilbert Achcar, "Marx et Engels face à la guerre", in Arnaud Spire, ed., *Marx contemporain*, Paris: Syllepse, 2003, pp. 171–84, especially 180ff.

45   Anderson, *Marx at the Margins*, p. 238.

46   Chandra, "Karl Marx, His Theories of Asian Societies and Colonial Rule", p. 409.

47   Frederick Engels, "Algeria", *Articles for The New American Cyclopaedia*, MECW, vol. 18, p. 67.

48   Karl Marx, *Capital Volume I*, MECW, vol. 35, p. 739.

49   Quoted in ibid.

50   Karl Marx, "Marx To Ferdinand Lassalle", MECW, vol. 40, p. 270.

51   See, for example, the excerpt from Marx's 1848 "Speech on the Question of Free Trade" quoted in the essay on "Marxism and Cosmopolitanism" published in this same collection, pp. 117–18.

52   Marx, *Capital Volume I*, p. 454. See Chandra, "Karl Marx, His Theories of Asian Societies and Colonial Rule", p. 439.

53   René Gallissot, *Marx, Marxisme et Algérie. Textes de Marx–Engels*, introduced and translated by René Gallissot in collaboration with Gilbert Badia, Paris: UGE 10/18, 1976, p. 183.

54   Karl Marx, Excerpts from M. M. Kovalevskij (Kovalevsky), *Obščinnoe Zemlevladenie*, in Lawrence Krader, *The Asiatic Mode of Production: Sources, Development and Critique in the Writings of Karl Marx*, Assen: Van Gorcum, 1975, p. 405. I checked this English translation against the French one in Gallissot (see note 53 above) in order to identify which passages constituted Marx's own comment on what he transcribed.

55   Ibid., p. 411.

56   Ibid., p. 412.

57   Ibid.

58   Karl Marx, "Drafts of the Letter to Vera Zasulich" and "Letter to Vera Zasulich", MECW, vol. 24, pp. 346–71.

59   In *Marx and the End of Orientalism*, Bryan Turner labelled these brands of Marxism "Hegelian Marxism". This is a rather misleading designation as various and quite contrasting aspects of the Hegelian legacy can be found in the history of Marxist thought.

60   Ibid., p. 85.

Marxism and Cosmopolitanism

In memory of a very dear friend, Peter Gowan

Four conceptions of cosmopolitanism

Four main conceptions of cosmopolitanism could be identified in Marx's time: philosophical (ethical); institutional (governmental); rights-based (juridical); and economic.

The oldest of these four variants was the philosophical:[1] it can be traced back to pre-Socratic thinkers, notably Heraclites, although the first explicit statement of the doctrine that used the word "cosmopolitan" itself is generally attributed to the most famous of the Cynics, Diogenes of Sinope. When asked his national affiliation, he is said to have replied: "a citizen of the world" (i.e. *kosmopolitês* ["cosmopolitan"]).[2]

Institutional cosmopolitanism, which argues in favour of a world government, was first plainly articulated in the early fourteenth century by Dante Alighieri, in his *De Monarchia*.[3] Dante pleaded for a world monarchy or empire, citing the Roman Empire as a model, with the achievement of "universal peace" as its major rationale. This vision found a radical counterpart in Anacharsis Cloots' advocacy in 1792 of a *République universelle* based on a social contract between individuals.[4]

Immanuel Kant issued the most famous statement on rights-based cosmopolitanism in his 1795 essay "Perpetual Peace: A Philosophical Sketch".[5] Kant made "cosmopolitan law" (*ius cosmopoliticum*, or *Weltbürgerrecht*) the last of his three definitive articles for perpetual peace, going beyond the "law of nations" (*ius gentium*, or international law) of which Hugo Grotius is the foremost exponent in legal history, as well as beyond the aspiration to establish a peaceful, rights-based society of states. Kant, however, restricted "cosmopolitan law" very explicitly to a single and rather banal entitlement to what he called "hospitality" (*Wirthbarkeit*), consisting of a right to visit (*Besuchsrecht*) – i.e. the right to a short-term sojourn, as distinct from the right to long-term or permanent settlement granted by invitation only (*Gastrecht*).[6] Although it is nowhere offered to the citizens of all countries under equal conditions, Kant's "cosmopolitan" right is actually recognised by most states nowadays as the right to short visits for various purposes such as tourism or business.

Kant also contributed to the topic of institutional cosmopolitanism. Although he considered that a world state or "state of nations" (*civitas gentium*) created as an act of free will would be the only rational way to overcome international anarchy, he believed it so unlikely that he advocated an international anti-war alliance instead of a universal republic. Kant observed that, as separate states are much preferable to the forceful fusion of states under a universal despotic monarchy, a federation of free states (*Föderalism freier Staaten*) would be the most realistic solution.

At the end of the "First Supplement" included in his treatise, Kant explained that the most efficient incentive for peace among nations is trade, i.e. money.[7] He thus adhered to the economic version of the theory of "liberal peace" after having emphasised its political variant: "republican peace" (the modern version of which is the theory of "democratic peace").[8] Kant thus showed his affinity with economic liberalism as articulated classically by his contemporary Adam Smith, whose *magnum opus* he had read.[9] Smith's 1776 *The Wealth of Nations*, while singing the praises of "free trade" and the "free circulation of labour and stock" as the safest way to opulence for all countries, also advocates low-cost (i.e. low-tax) government as a necessary correlate if states wish capital to remain freely on their territory. Within the context of this argument, he invoked the concept of cosmopolitanism without the term itself, but with its English equivalent, defining it as an attribute of capitalists:

> The proprietor of stock is properly a *citizen of the world*, and is not necessarily attached to any particular country. He would be apt to abandon the country in which he was exposed to a vexatious inquisition, in order to be assessed to a burdensome tax, and would remove his stock to some other country where he could either carry on his business, or enjoy his fortune more at his ease.[10]

The concept and the term itself were harshly attacked by Smith's principal bourgeois critic, Friedrich List, in his *The National System of Political Economy* (1841).[11] Setting "political economy" against "cosmopolitical economy" (*kosmopolitische Ökonomie*), List criticised the "philanthropy and cosmopolitanism" of British liberal economists acrimoniously, denouncing their "free trade" attitude as stemming in reality from the dominant position of their country and deriding their French and German co-thinkers as naive. An heir to mercantilism and a major exponent of economic nationalism and protectionism, List emphasised the duty of each nation to put its own selfish interests above any other consideration and principle. He is one of the first authors to use the label "cosmopolitan" pejoratively and was, in his day, the most prominent critic of cosmopolitanism. In his book he called it *bodenloser Kosmopolitismus*,[12] by which he clearly meant "rootless" – i.e. having no sense of belonging to a country – or unpatriotic; this same connotation of *Boden* ("soil") would find its way into the late nineteenth-century German nationalist formula, *Blut und Boden* ("blood and soil"). Cosmopolitanism, as List described it, "neither recognises the principle of nationality, nor takes into consideration the satisfaction of its interests".[13]

The concept of cosmopolitanism, and the term itself, would re-emerge in the economic literature in neutral guise, in the 1848 textbook *Principles of Political Economy* authored by John Stuart Mill, a disciple of Smith and David Ricardo:

> [C]apital is becoming more and more cosmopolitan; there is so much greater similarity of manners and institutions than formerly, and so much less alienation of feeling, among the more civilized countries, that both population and capital now move from one of those countries to another on much less temptation than heretofore.[14]

Mill was more realistic than Smith, however, in acknowledging the limits to the circulation of capital in his time. He commented:

> It needs but a small motive to transplant capital, or even persons, from Warwickshire to Yorkshire; but a much greater to make them remove to India, the colonies, or Ireland. ... To countries still barbarous, or, like Russia or Turkey, only beginning to be civilized, capital will not migrate, unless under the inducement of a very great extra profit.[15]

Marx and Engels' initial conception of cosmopolitanism

In his 1841 doctoral dissertation on the philosophies of nature of Democritus and Epicurus, Marx did not comment on the elements of egalitarianism or cosmopolitan ethics in the thinking of the two ancient Greek philosophers. Only two years later, after his political radicalisation, did Marx approach the theme of cosmopolitanism – albeit indirectly – in relation to a critique of the bourgeois transformation of the world. That was in his contribution to the criticism of religion, which he regarded as "the premise of all criticism".[16]

Infamous because of its anti-Jewish utterances, which are particularly unbearable to modern ears,[17] Marx's 1843 pamphlet *On the Jewish Question* is nevertheless a landmark in his transition to historical materialism and communism. Marx criticised Judaism all the more harshly as he himself was of Jewish origin, and hence felt at ease in his severity. Behind his stereotyped Hegel-like depiction of "the Jew", who is presumed to have no homeland but money (a prejudice applied throughout history to all diasporic communities specialising in merchant and money-lending activities), Marx's real target was the global reign of money, especially among "Christian peoples". He meant this not in the anti-Semitic sense of Jewish control over the world, but in that Christians themselves "have become Jews". Marx was thus directly rebutting the theologian Bruno Bauer who, in his critique of Judaism, had praised a conception of Christianity inspired by Ludwig Feuerbach.[18]

> The Jew has emancipated himself in a Jewish manner, not only because he has acquired financial power, but also because, through him and also apart from him, *money* has become

a world power and the practical Jewish spirit has become the practical spirit of the Christian nations. The Jews have emancipated themselves insofar as the Christians have become Jews. ... The god of the Jews has become secularised and has become the god of the world. The bill of exchange is the real god of the Jew. His god is only an illusory bill of exchange.[19]

Cosmopolitanism (world citizenship, *Weltbürgertum*) being a global extension of the concept of citizenship,[20] note that Marx, in his *On the Jewish Question*, does not reject the political concept of "citizen"; on the contrary, he upholds it against the abstract notion of Man (*Mensch*).[21] In the use made of the latter in the declarations of rights issued by successive bourgeois revolutions, he sees a codename for a member of "civil society" (*bürgerliche Gesellschaft*), i.e. a bourgeois:

> Above all, we note the fact that the so-called rights of man, the *droits de l'homme* as distinct from the *droits du citoyen*, are nothing but the rights of a *member of civil society* – i.e., the rights of egoistic man, of man separated from other men and from the community. ...
>
> This fact becomes still more puzzling when we see that the political emancipators go so far as to reduce citizenship, and the *political community*, to a mere means for maintaining these so-called rights of man, that, therefore, the *citoyen* is declared to be the servant of egoistic *homme*, that the sphere in which man acts as a communal being is degraded to a level below the sphere in which he acts as a partial being, and that, finally, it is not man as *citoyen*, but man as *bourgeois* who is considered to be the *essential* and *true* man.[22]

In the 1844 Introduction to his *Contribution to the Critique of Hegel's Philosophy of Law*, written immediately after *On the Jewish Question*, Marx no longer deals just with Judaism but with religion in general and Christianity in particular. There appears the messianic notion of the proletariat as the saviour of humanity – a secular alternative to Jesus, the Christian messiah. The proletariat is described in Christian-like terms as a class that "has a universal character by its universal suffering" and "which can no longer invoke a *historical* but only a *human* title".[23] It is a class endowed, therefore, with a worldwide mission: "By proclaiming the *dissolution of the hitherto existing world order* the proletariat merely states the *secret of its own existence*, for it *is in fact* the dissolution of that world order."[24]

Whereas Marx states in this Introduction that "the *criticism of religion* [turns] into the *criticism of law* and the *criticism of theology* into the *criticism of politics*",[25] it is actually to the critique of political economy that he applied himself in the wake of critiquing Hegel's *Philosophy of Law*. This was due in large part to his enthusiastic reading of Engels' pioneering *Outlines of a Critique of Political Economy* – a short 1843 text that had a tremendous influence on Marx's own intellectual trajectory, and which he described in the famous Preface to his own 1859 *Contribution to the Critique of Political Economy* as a "sketch of genius" (*geniale Skizze*).[26]

In his *Outlines*, Engels – who was already familiar with political economy (he cites Smith, Ricardo, List, Jean-Baptiste Say, James Mill and Thomas Malthus among others) – composed the first communist critique of capitalist cosmopolitanism as represented above all by Smith, whom he calls "the economic Luther", describing his doctrine as "Protestant hypocrisy [that] took the place of Catholic candour".[27] The young Engels denounces vehemently the hypocrisy of liberal cosmopolitanism and its "philanthropy" – a direct echo of List's critique, to which he refers explicitly,[28] as well as an echo of his own earlier German-nationalist criticism of liberal cosmopolitanism.[29]

> Thus economics took on a philanthropic character. ... It affected a solemn abhorrence of the bloody terror of the mercantile system, and proclaimed trade to be a bond of friendship and union among nations as among individuals. All was pure splendour and magnificence – yet the premises reasserted themselves soon enough, and in contrast to this sham philanthropy produced the Malthusian population theory – the crudest, most barbarous theory that ever existed, a system of despair which struck down all those beautiful phrases about philanthropy and world citizenship. The premises begot and reared the factory system and modern slavery, which yields nothing in inhumanity and cruelty to ancient slavery. Modern economics – the system of free trade based on Adam Smith's *Wealth of Nations* – reveals itself to be that same hypocrisy, inconsistency and immorality which now confront free humanity in every sphere.[30]
>
> Such is the humanity of trade. And this hypocritical way of misusing morality for immoral purposes is the pride of the free trade system. "Have we not overthrown the barbarism of the monopolies?" exclaim the hypocrites. "Have we not carried civilisation to distant parts of the world? Have we not brought about the fraternisation of the peoples, and reduced the number of wars?" Yes, all this you have done – but *how!* *You* have destroyed the small monopolies so that the *one* great basic monopoly, property, may function the more freely and unrestrictedly. You have civilised the ends of the earth to win new terrain for the deployment of your vile avarice. You have brought about the fraternisation of the peoples – but the

fraternity is the fraternity of thieves. You have reduced the number of wars – to earn all the bigger profits in peace, to intensify to the utmost the enmity between individuals, the ignominious war of competition![31]

However bitter Engels' criticism of liberal cosmopolitanism was, he no longer condoned mercantilist nationalism in the *Outlines*. Instead, he expressed a view that later became central to his and Marx's theory: that despite its brutality, capitalist cosmopolitanism fulfils a progressive historical role, laying the groundwork for a higher level of universalism.

> But was Smith's system, then, not an advance? Of course it was, and a necessary advance at that. It was necessary to overthrow the mercantile system with its monopolies and hindrances to trade, so that the true consequences of private property could come to light. It was necessary for all these petty, local and national considerations to recede into the background, so that the struggle of our time could become a universal human struggle.[32]

Starting in Paris in late 1843, Marx embarked in his turn on the intensive study of political economy through the works of its major British and French representatives. This thematic conversion led him to echo Engels' criticism of capitalist cosmopolitanism in his *Economic and Philosophic Manuscripts of 1844*:

> This political economy begins by seeming to acknowledge man (his independence, spontaneity, etc.); then, locating private property in man's own being, it can no longer be conditioned by the local, national or other *characteristics of private property* as of *something existing outside itself*. This political economy,

consequently, displays a *cosmopolitan*, universal energy which overthrows every restriction and bond so as to establish itself instead as the *sole* politics, the sole universality, the sole limit and sole bond. Hence it must throw aside this *hypocrisy* in the course of its further development and come *out in its complete cynicism*.[33]

In 1845, Marx drafted a devastating critique of List's *The National System of Political Economy*, in which he counterposed German bourgeois nationalism with a first formulation of the theme of a proletariat with no nationality but its class condition:

> What then does the German philistine want? He wants to be a *bourgeois*, an exploiter, inside the country, but he wants also not to be exploited outside the country. He puffs himself up into being the "nation" in relation to foreign countries and says: I do not submit to the laws of competition; that is contrary to my national dignity; as the nation I am a being superior to huckstering.
>
> The nationality of the worker is neither French, nor English, nor German, it is *labour, free slavery, self-huckstering*. His government is neither French, nor English, nor German, it is capital. His native air is neither French, nor German, nor English, it is factory air.[34]

In their co-authored *The German Ideology*, which they started writing later in 1845, Marx and Engels applied to the philosophical realm their criticism of their compatriots' hypocritical cosmopolitanism (as opposed to true cosmopolitanism). They submitted Bruno Bauer and Max Stirner in particular to vitriolic irony, debunking the German chauvinism behind their theoretical arrogance: "Herr Venedey is a cosmopolitan compared with the Saints

Bruno and Max, who, in the universal dominance of theory, proclaim the universal dominance of Germany."[35] In criticising Stirner's Hegelian view, according to which social relations are fostered by philosophical concepts, Marx and Engels underlined the fact that "free competition and world trade gave birth to hypocritical, bourgeois cosmopolitanism and the notion of man ..."[36]

They despised Kant as the philosophical expression of the German bourgeoisie's impotence compared to its French and English counterparts: "These petty, local interests had as their counterpart, on the one hand, the truly local and provincial narrow-mindedness of the German burghers and, on the other hand, their cosmopolitan swollen-headedness."[37] Quoting from Heinrich Heine's famous satirical verse-epic *Deutschland. Ein Wintermärchen* (*Germany: A Winter's Tale*), Marx and Engels pointed one more time in their long manuscript to "the narrowly national outlook which underlies the alleged universalism and cosmopolitanism of the Germans".[38]

Against this hypocritical cosmopolitanism, they stressed the true universalism of the world proletariat that stems from its material condition:

> Modern universal intercourse cannot be controlled by individuals, unless it is controlled by all. This appropriation is further determined by the manner in which it must be effected. It can only be effected through a union, which by the character of the proletariat itself can again only be a universal one, and through a revolution, in which, on the one hand, the power of the earlier mode of production and intercourse and social organisation is overthrown, and, on the other hand, there develops the universal character and the energy of the proletariat, which are required to accomplish the appropriation ...[39]

In another statement that Marx had written on the margin of the manuscript, we find a powerful and premonitory description of capitalist global development and worldwide proletarian struggle as prerequisites for communism:

> This "*estrangement*" [*Entfremdung*, i.e. alienation] (to use a term which will be comprehensible to the philosophers) can, of course, only be abolished given two *practical* premises. In order to become an "unendurable" power, i.e. a power against which men make a revolution, it must necessarily have rendered the great mass of humanity "propertyless," and moreover in contradiction to an existing world of wealth and culture; both these premises presuppose a great increase in productive power, a high degree of its development.
>
> And, on the other hand, this development of productive forces (which at the same time implies the actual empirical existence of men in their *world-historical*, instead of local, being) is an absolutely necessary practical premise, because without it privation, *want* is merely made general, and with *want* the struggle for necessities would begin again, and all the old filthy business would necessarily be restored; and furthermore, because only with this universal development of productive forces is a universal intercourse between men established, which on the one side produces in all nations simultaneously the phenomenon of the "propertyless" mass (universal competition), makes each nation dependent on the revolutions of the others, and finally puts *world-historical*, empirically universal individuals in place of local ones. ... The proletariat can thus only exist *world-historically*, just as communism, its activity, can only have a "world-historical" existence.[40]

The contrast between hypocritical bourgeois cosmopolitanism and the true cosmopolitanism of the proletariat informs Engels' 1846 article on the "Festival of Nations" in London:

> The fraternisation of nations, as it is now being carried out everywhere by the extreme proletarian party in contrast to the old instinctive national egoism and to the hypocritical private-egotistical cosmopolitanism of free trade, is worth more than all the German theories of true socialism put together.[41]
>
> Communist as well as cosmopolitan principles were already voiced at this festival of August 10; ... The main credit for the organisation of this cosmopolitan festival was his [George Julian Harney's] ...[42]

This is also the case with Engels' 1847 mockery of Louis Blanc's chauvinistic "cosmopolitanism":

> A Frenchman is necessarily a cosmopolite [says Louis Blanc]. Yes, in a world ruled over by French influence, French manners, fashions, ideas, politics. In a world in which every nation has adopted the characteristics of French nationality. But that is exactly what the democrats of other nations will not like. Quite ready to give up the harshness of their own nationality, they expect the same from the French. They will not be satisfied in the assertion, on the part of the French, that they *are* cosmopolites; assertion which amounts to the demand urged upon all others to become Frenchmen.[43]

The maturation of Marx and Engels' conception of cosmopolitanism

From 1848 on, the issue of bourgeois and proletarian cosmo-politanism is no longer addressed in Marx and Engels' writings through its philosophical or right-based variant. It is viewed instead through the lenses of historical materialism, i.e. through their analysis of worldwide capitalist development, with bourgeois cosmopolitanism as its ideological accompaniment and the development of the proletariat as a universal class, bearer of the global communist future, as its corollary. The term "cosmopolitanism" itself seldom appears in Marx and Engels' later writings; most often, but not exclusively, it is used with regard to capitalist cosmopolitanism.

Its first occurrence is, by far, the most famous: in the cele-brated section of the *Manifesto of the Communist Party*, the two authors write an ode to the capitalist transformation of the world that rings very much like one of the praises of "globalisation" that proliferated during the 1990s:

> The bourgeoisie has through its exploitation of the world market given a cosmopolitan character to production and consumption in every country. To the great chagrin of Reactionists, it has drawn from under the feet of industry the national ground on which it stood. All old-established national industries have been destroyed or are daily being destroyed. They are dislodged by new industries, whose introduction becomes a life and death question for all civilised nations, by industries that no longer work up indigenous raw material, but raw material drawn from the remotest zones; industries whose products are consumed, not only at home, but in every quarter of the globe. In place of the old wants, satisfied by

the production of the country, we find new wants, requiring for their satisfaction the products of distant lands and climes. In place of the old local and national seclusion and self-sufficiency, we have intercourse in every direction, universal inter-dependence of nations. And as in material, so also in intellectual production. The intellectual creations of individual nations become common property. National one-sidedness and narrow-mindedness become more and more impossible, and from the numerous national and local literatures, there arises a world literature.[44]

This eloquent passage is actually indicative of Marx and Engels' positivist illusion at that time regarding the progressive role of worldwide capitalist expansion – their adherence, albeit critical, to the view that advocates of imperialism, later in the nineteenth century, will call the "civilising mission" of economically-advanced states. It took the two founders of historical materialism a few more years before they started reaching a more complex and dialectical view of the global role of capitalism: the huge cost of its plunder of agrarian economies and the contradictory effect of its export of industrial means in order to subjugate non-industrialised countries to the needs of capitalist metropolises, thus impeding their development according to their own needs.

There is, however, an interesting insight in this regard in Marx's famous 1848 "Speech on the Question of Free Trade":

For instance, we are told that free trade would create an international division of labor, and thereby give to each country the production which is most in harmony with its natural advantage.

You believe, perhaps, gentlemen, that the production of coffee and sugar is the natural destiny of the West Indies.

Two centuries ago, nature, which does not trouble itself about commerce, had planted neither sugar-cane nor coffee trees there. And it may be that in less than half a century you will find there neither coffee nor sugar, for the East Indies, by means of cheaper production, have already successfully broken down this so-called natural destiny of the West Indies.

And the West Indies, with their natural wealth, are as heavy a burden for England as the weavers of Dacca, who also were destined from the beginning of time to weave by hand.[45]

Nevertheless, the positivist faith in linear progress that Marx and Engels held in 1848 is at the root of the unbound optimism they displayed at the same time with regard to the prospects of proletarian revolution – an optimism that will be severely dampened two decades later by the bloody suppression of the 1871 Paris Commune.[46] The same faith in progress informs the description of the proletarian-communist struggle in a much-discussed passage of the *Manifesto*, where Marx and Engels reply implicitly to the accusation of cosmopolitanism (as opposed to patriotism) made against the communists:

> The working men have no country. We cannot take from them what they have not got. Since the proletariat must first of all acquire political supremacy, must rise to be the national class [the leading class of the nation[47]], must constitute itself *the* nation, it is so far, itself national, though not in the bourgeois sense of the word.
>
> National differences and antagonism between peoples are daily more and more vanishing, owing to the development of the bourgeoisie, to freedom of commerce, to the world market, to uniformity in the mode of production and in the conditions of life corresponding thereto.

The supremacy of the proletariat will cause them to vanish still faster. United action, of the leading civilised countries at least, is one of the first conditions for the emancipation of the proletariat.

In proportion as the exploitation of one individual by another is put an end to, the exploitation of one nation by another will also be put an end to. In proportion as the antagonism between classes within the nation vanishes, the hostility of one nation to another will come to an end.[48]

The standard English translation of the *Manifesto*'s famous sentence "*Die Arbeiter haben kein Vaterland*" as "The working men have no country" can be misleading. A clearer translation of that sentence would be: "The workers have no homeland." The original term *Vaterland* – literally, "fatherland" – is actually a reminiscence of Heine's well-known poem on the 1844 Silesian weavers' uprising, the *Weberlied*. Engels translated that poem into English; here is his translation of the relevant stanza: "A curse to the false fatherland / That has nothing for us but distress and shame / Where we suffered hunger and misery / We are weaving thy shroud, Old Germany!"[49]

From the above-quoted passage from the *Manifesto* flows the view that the conquest of power by the proletariat turns it from a class without homeland or "fatherland" into a "national class", a class that embodies the nation, albeit in harmony with other proletarian-led nations. However, a key statement that comes before that passage in the *Manifesto*, at the beginning of the same chapter, assigns a special role to the Communists in that regard. Too often overlooked,[50] it must be borne in mind in order to properly understand Marx and Engels' conception:

> The Communists are distinguished from the other working-class parties by this only: 1. In the national struggles of the proletarians of the different countries, they point out and bring to the front the common interests of the entire proletariat, independently of all nationality. 2. In the various stages of development which the struggle of the working class against the bourgeoisie has to pass through, they always and everywhere represent the interests of the movement as a whole.[51]

This statement makes it clear that Marx and Engels regarded the Communists as the political representatives of the proletariat's objective universalism/cosmopolitanism, which is therefore not the spontaneous and common subjective consciousness of the whole class. Pheng Cheah overlooks this dialectic of the objective and subjective (another version of the well-known dialectic of the class *in itself* and the class *for itself*) when he asserts the following:

> For Marx, proletarian cosmopolitanism is no longer just a normative horizon of world history or a matter of right growing out of international commerce. It is a necessary and existing form of solidarity grounded in the global exploitation that has resulted from the global development of forces of production. ...
>
> Because universal exploitation creates a universal class in advanced countries that has been dispossessed and freed of any illusions by utter poverty, the bourgeois ideology of "humanity" will be demystified and bourgeois cosmopolitanism will be sublated (*aufgehoben*) and replaced by the cosmopolitan solidarity of the proletariat.[52]

The rise to power of the class or the illusion of its partaking in political power, i.e. in the "ownership" of the nation, can lead it to succumb to nationalism – or patriotism (from *patria*, the "fatherland") – as in the case of the French small-holding peasantry whose ideology Marx described sarcastically in his 1852 *The Eighteenth Brumaire of Louis Bonaparte*:

> The army was the "*point d'honneur*" of the small-holding peasants, it was they themselves transformed into heroes, defending their new possessions against the outer world, glorifying their recently won nationhood, plundering and revolutionizing the world. The uniform was their own state dress; war was their poetry; the smallholding, extended and rounded off in imagination, was their fatherland, and patriotism the ideal form of their sense of property.[53]

Likewise, in his writings on the 1870 Franco-German war, Marx castigated the toilers' patriotism on both sides. In one of the sentences he added to the German translation of his "Second Address of the General Council of the International Workingmen's Association on the Franco-Prussian War" – after the prophecy that "Decimated by the battles abroad, [German labourers] will be once more decimated by misery at home"[54] – he made the following comment, demeaning the patriots' complaint about capitalist cosmopolitanism itself: "And the patriotic clamourers will say, to comfort them, that capital has no [fatherland] and that wages are regulated by the *non-patriotic international* law of demand and supply."[55]

Marx had no sympathy for this "patriotic" denigration of capitalist cosmopolitanism, which he considered an expression of a petit-bourgeois mindset. The above-mentioned additional sentence is followed by this comment: "Is it, therefore, not the high time for the German working class to raise its voice and no longer allow the gentlemen of the middle class to speak *in its name*?"[56]

Marx's critique of capitalist cosmopolitanism remained a denunciation of its capitalist substance and not a condemnation of cosmopolitanism *per se*. In the remarkable criticism of the Yankee (capitalist) universalism of Henry Charles Carey included in his 1857–58 *Grundrisse*, Marx sketches, indirectly and briefly, a view of an alternative universalism that acknowledges national differences – one of those countless insights in his work that, regrettably, he did not develop:

> Carey's generality is Yankee universality. For him, France and China are equally near. He is at all times the man who lives both on the Atlantic and the Pacific coast. … Carey, as a true Yankee, absorbs from all directions the abundant material which the Old World offers him, not indeed to cognise the immanent soul of this material and thus to concede to it its right to its own proper life, but to work it up as lifeless pieces of evidence, as indifferent matter, for his own purposes, i.e. for the propositions derived from his Yankee point of view.[57]

Indeed, Marx's most thorough analysis of capitalist cosmopolitanism, which is included in his 1859 *Contribution to the Critique of Political Economy*, testifies to this double-edged character: a positive assessment of capitalist cosmopolitanism's supersession of all sorts of barriers erected between human beings in previous epochs, and of its practical rationality as well, along with derision of the limitations of this cosmopolitanism that dissolves world "citizenship" into world "civil society" – to borrow the terms of *On the Jewish Question*, the trace of which is palpable in what follows – or in other words, into the market.

> As money develops into world money, so the commodity owner becomes a cosmopolitan. The cosmopolitan relations of

men to one another originally comprise only their relations as commodity owners. Commodities as such are indifferent to all religious, political, national and linguistic barriers. Their universal language is price and their common bond is money. But together with the development of world money as against national coins, there develops the commodity owner's cosmopolitanism, a cult of practical reason, in opposition to the traditional religious, national and other prejudices which impede the metabolic process of mankind. ... The sublime idea in which for him the whole world merges is that of a market, the world market.[58]

Cosmopolitanism and internationalism

Nowhere in Marx and Engels' writings is the concept of "internationalism" opposed politically to that of "cosmopolitanism". While it is true that, in *The Civil War in France*, which he wrote in 1871 as an "Address of the General Council of the International Working Men's Association", Marx counterpoised "the international counter-organization of labour" to "the cosmopolitan conspiracy of capital", this was only and clearly a stylistic choice in order to avoid the repetition of "international". This latter word had already been used twice in the same sentence, the first time in relation to the bourgeoisie. (Here is the whole sentence: "While the European governments thus testify, before Paris, to the international character of class rule, they cry down the International Working Men's Association – the international counter-organization of labour against the cosmopolitan conspiracy of capital – as the head fountain of all these disasters.")[59]

Internationalism was not a moral category or a vague political principle for Marx and Engels, but a direct reference to the

International as an organisation. This is clear from the first occurrence of the term in their publications, in their vitriolic booklet against Mikhail Bakunin written mainly by Engels together with Paul Lafargue in 1873. First published in French, the booklet derides a Bakunin who "since 1868 has played the internationalist"[60] – which is a reference to the fact that he joined the International Working Men's Association (IWMA) that year. A few pages before that, the attribute "cosmopolitan" is related to the proletariat itself (in the French original): the IWMA's mission, according to the booklet, consisted in "uniting [the working class] into a single whole and making the ruling classes and their governments feel for the first time the [cosmopolitan] power of the proletariat."[61]

A similar use of the attribute *cosmopolitan* appears one year later in a letter from Engels to Friedrich Adolph Sorge, after the latter's resignation from the General Council of the IWMA:

> With your resignation the *old* International is entirely wound up and at an end. And that is a good thing. It belonged to the period of the Second Empire, when the oppression throughout Europe prescribed unity and abstention from all internal controversy for the workers' movement, then just reawakening. It was the moment when the common, cosmopolitan interests of the proletariat could come to the fore.[62]

Soon afterwards, in a speech he gave in London in 1875 in support of the Poles' struggle, Marx stressed that they are "the only European people that has fought and is fighting as the *cosmopolitan soldier of the revolution*".[63]

Internationalism was indeed Marx and Engels' own version of institutional cosmopolitanism: always reluctant to speculate about the hypothetical communist future and reinvent the world

(Marx did not even bother to discuss the Paris Commune's advocacy of a *République universelle*, although he discussed in detail other components of its programme), they preferred to dedicate themselves to subverting it, focusing their attention on the actual implementation of the cosmopolitan principle in the international organisation of workers. "Perpetual" world peace, as they saw it, could not be achieved by treaties, alliances or federation schemes of any sort between bourgeois states, but only by the worldwide victory of the proletarian revolution. In the messages exchanged between the IWMA branches on both sides of the Franco–Prussian War, Marx saw proof that

> in contrast to old society, with its economic miseries and its political delirium, a new society is springing up, whose international rule will be *Peace*, because its national ruler will be everywhere the same – *Labour*! The pioneer of that new society is the International Working Men's Association.[64]

Shortly after the IWMA – for all intents and purposes – expired, Marx vehemently criticised the reduction of "internationalism" to a vague moral concept in place of the practical concept whose supreme embodiment remained, in his view, the international organisation of the working class, even though the existing (first) International was agonising. This was in his famous 1875 comments on the draft copy of the Gotha Programme of the German Social Democratic Party, which his German socialist friends had sent him:

> Lassalle, in opposition to the *Communist Manifesto* and to all earlier socialism, conceived the workers' movement from the narrowest national standpoint. He is being followed in this – and that after the work of the International!

It is altogether self-evident that, to be able to fight at all, the working class must organize itself at home *as a class* and that its own country is the immediate arena of its struggle. To this extent its class struggle is national, not in substance, but, as the *Communist Manifesto* says, "in form". But the "framework of the present-day national state", for instance, the German Empire, is itself, in its turn, economically "within the framework of the world market", politically "within the framework of the system of states". Every businessman knows that German trade is at the same time foreign trade, and the greatness of Mr. Bismarck consists, to be sure, precisely in his pursuing his kind of *international* policy.

And to what does the German Workers' Party reduce its internationalism? To the consciousness that the result of its efforts "will be the international brotherhood of peoples" – a phrase borrowed from the bourgeois League of Peace and Freedom, which is intended to pass as equivalent to the international brotherhood of working classes in the joint struggle against the ruling classes and their governments. So not a word about the *international functions* of the German working class! And it is thus that it is to defy its own bourgeoisie – which is already linked up in brotherhood against it with the bourgeois of all other countries – and Mr. Bismarck's international policy of conspiracy!

In fact, the internationalism of the program stands *even infinitely below* that of the Free Trade party. The latter also asserts that the result of its efforts will be "the international brotherhood of peoples". But it also *does* something to make trade international and by no means contents itself with the consciousness – that all people are carrying on trade at home.

The international activity of the working classes does not in any way depend on the existence of the "International Working

Men's Association". This was only the first attempt to create a central organ for the activity; an attempt which was a lasting success on account of the impulse which it gave, but which was no longer realisable in *its first historical form* after the fall of the Paris Commune.

Bismarck's *Norddeutsche* was absolutely right when it announced, to the satisfaction of its master, that the German Workers' Party had forsworn internationalism in the new programme.[65]

For this same reason, after the First International came into existence and with the subsequent rise of other types of international networks of working-class organisations,[66] "internationalism" became the key term used to designate the practical solidarity of the world proletariat instead of the vague "cosmopolitanism". Even so, the latter term was not reserved by Marx and Engels as exclusive to the bourgeoisie; nor, as we have seen, was it turned into a pejorative attribute *per se*, but used as a complementary term, especially when the use of "internationalism" was not appropriate. In his well-known 1978 polemic against Eugen Dühring, Engels sings the praises of cultural cosmopolitanism as opposed to the national narrow-mindedness of his and Marx's adversary:

The national narrow-mindedness of modern man is still much too cosmopolitan for Herr Dühring. He wants also to do away with the two levers which in the world as it is today give at least the opportunity of rising above the narrow national standpoint: knowledge of the ancient languages, which opens a wider common horizon at least to those people of various nationalities who have had a classical education; and knowledge of modern languages, through the medium of which alone the people of different nations can make themselves understood by one another and acquaint themselves with what is happening beyond their own borders.[67]

"Cosmopolitanism" after Marx and Engels: Kautsky, Gramsci and the Comintern

Nor was "cosmopolitanism" as such an issue in Marxist debate after Marx and Engels. One hardly finds occurrences of the term in the documents of the Second and Third Internationals, and in the contemporary writings of their key leading members – or, for that matter, in the contemporary writings of independent or dissident Marxists.

Karl Kautsky used the term, whether directly or indirectly, in his works on the history of religion: it appears in his 1908 *Foundations of Christianity* in a sentence of a passage that Kautsky quotes from Theodor Mommsen's *magnum opus*, *The History of Rome* (a multi-volume work that, in 1902, earned its author the second-ever Nobel Prize for Literature). The citation is included in the third part – on "The Jews" – of Kautsky's book;[68] it is useful to reproduce here Mommsen's sentence where the word appears, as it sheds some light on subsequent developments involving the same term:

> Even in the ancient world Judaism was an effective leaven of cosmopolitanism and of national decomposition, and to that extent a specially privileged member in the Caesarian state, the polity of which was strictly speaking nothing but a citizenship of the world, and the nationality of which was at bottom nothing but humanity.[69]

There was nothing anti-Semitic or even pejorative in this statement (Mommsen had been one of the founders, in 1890, of the *Verein zur Abwehr des Antisemitismus* [Association for the Defence against Anti-Semitism]), nor in Kautsky's quoting of the sentence. Neither reserved the term for the Jews, in fact: they applied it to different cases, associating it at times with humanism. In his 1888 book *Thomas More and His Utopia*, Kautsky applied the term to the Catholic Church, contrasting its universalist cosmopolitanism with commercial cosmopolitanism, which went along dialectically with the development of the nation-state and nationalism:

> In the Middle Ages we find a narrow particularism, a parochial outlook side by side with a cosmopolitanism which comprised the whole of Western Christendom. The feeling of nationality was therefore very weak. ...
>
> Commerce put in place of local ties a cosmopolitan feeling which was at home wherever a profit could be earned. At the same time it set up nationality against the universality of the Church. World trade widened the horizon of the Western peoples far beyond the region of the Catholic Church, and simultaneously narrowed it within the sphere of their own nation.[70]

Likewise, Gramsci – certainly the pre-1939 Marxist author who made the most extensive use of the term "cosmopolitanism" and its derivatives, in his *Prison Notebooks*[71] – employed it repeatedly as an attribute of universal religions in general and Christianity in particular, but also of a number of other empires or ideologies. However, Gramsci's thoughts on the issue of cosmopolitanism are mainly integral to his political sociology of Italian intellectuals and, secondarily, that of the intellectuals of other major European nations, although he also attempted at times to apply the concept to non-European cases.[72]

Gramsci underlined the fact that Italy is the territory with the longest historical tradition of cosmopolitanism – from that of the Roman Empire to that of the Catholic Church – and saw in the "cosmopolitan" legacy common to Italy and Germany (the Holy Roman Empire of the German Nation) the reason behind the delay of their national unity, as a result of the paucity of national intellectuals and the historical dominance of "cosmopolitan intellectuals" in both countries.

At a time when Italy and Germany were prey to ultranationalist movements and when he himself was incarcerated by Italian Fascism, Gramsci was preoccupied with the historical trend and wondered in the *Prison Notebooks* whether or not the over-the-top momentum of the national awakening in his country had been a natural result of its belatedness, and whether or not it was, moreover, durable. He tried to reassure himself – not without an obvious measure of wishful thinking – in terms very much in line with the Marxian tradition where cosmopolitanism is positively connoted against nationalism, and superseded by internationalism as its modern proletarian form:

> *Must* the national movement that led to the unification of the Italian State necessarily issue in nationalism and nationalistic and military imperialism? Such an outcome is anachronistic and unhistorical; it is actually against all of Italy's traditions, the Roman first, and then the Catholic. These traditions are cosmopolitan. That the national movement should react against the traditions and give rise to a nationalism of intellectuals can be explained, but this is not an organic-popular reaction … Italian cosmopolitanism cannot but become internationalism. Not the world-citizen, as a Roman or a Catholic, but as a worker and producer of civilisation. So it can be argued that the Italian tradition is dialectically continued by the working

people and their intellectuals, not by the traditional citizen and the traditional intellectual. Of all peoples, the Italian people is "nationally" the most interested in internationalism. Not only the worker, but also the peasant and especially the southern peasant ... The Italian people's civilising mission lies in the revival of Roman and medieval cosmopolitanism, but in its most modern and advanced form.[73]

In the documents of the Communist International, the institutional conception of cosmopolitanism is pervasive, albeit without the presence of the word itself. During the revolutionary turmoil of the immediate aftermath of the First World War, with the hardline left-wing and overenthusiastic positions that characterised its initial years, the Comintern made several programmatic statements about the shape of the post-revolutionary world, with disparities stemming from the lack of proper discussion of the issue.

Already in the "Platform" adopted at its First Congress in 1919, the International stated that the working class must "abolish State frontiers" and "change the entire world into one cooperative community",[74] while denouncing the League of Nations (then in gestation) as a counter-revolutionary capitalist and imperialist coalition. Against the latter, and against bourgeois cosmopolitanism in general, the "Theses on the International Situation" adopted by the same congress declare: "Instead of the slogan of an international union of revolutionary workers' republics, the slogan of an international association of sham democracies is put forward ..."[75] The 1919 "May Day Manifesto" of the Comintern's Executive Committee (ECCI) ends with the prediction that "In 1920 the great International Soviet Republic will come to birth."[76] The "Statutes of the Communist International" adopted at its Second Congress in 1920 reiterate the call for "the creation of an international Soviet republic", defining it as "a transitional stage to the complete abolition of the State".[77]

With the defeat of the post-war revolutionary wave, a shift occurred towards a defensive position, with a new emphasis on "the fight against fascism and war and for the united front", as well as "for Soviet Russia", as stated in the 1923 "May Day Manifesto". A new principle appears in the documents – one that will become increasingly unconditional until the demise of the Comintern: "[I]t is the duty of all class-conscious workers to declare themselves unreservedly for Soviet Russia."[78] However, the July 1924 Manifesto on the tenth anniversary of the outbreak of the war, written by Leon Trotsky and adopted by the Fifth Congress of the Comintern, ends on a note that prefigures its author's bitter opposition to the doctrine of "socialism in one country" that would prevail soon after:

> If Soviet Russia was able over a number of years to stand out against capitalist Europe and America together, the victory of the European proletariat will be the more certain when, after capturing power, the States of Europe come together in a Soviet Federation, the United Workers' and Peasants' States of Europe. …
>
> The European Socialist Federation will in this way become the corner-stone of the Socialist World Republic.[79]

The new Statutes adopted at the Fifth Congress state that the Comintern fights "for the foundation of a world union of Socialist Soviet Republics".[80] The USSR had been created in 1922 with a view to extending the Union to the whole world: hence the absence of a national reference in its name (only years later did "Soviet" become a national label). The theses on the international situation adopted by the ECCI in December 1926, and introduced by Nikolai Bukharin, reproduce the perspective laid out in the 1924 Manifesto: "as against Pan-Europa, the Socialist United States of Europe; as against the League of Nations, a Union of Socialist Soviet Republics".[81] Likewise, the new Statutes adopted at the 1928 Sixth Congress stipulate that the Comintern "fights for the establishment of the world dictatorship of the proletariat, for the establishment of a World Union of Socialist Soviet Republics …"[82] In this early phase of the left-wing communist "Third Period" of the Comintern, the Sixth Congress adopted a long "Programme of the Communist International", also introduced by Bukharin, where a blueprint for the transition to world communism is set out:

> Once centres of socialism exist, in the form of Socialist Soviet Republics with steadily growing economic power, the colonies which have broken away from imperialism draw nearer, economically, to the industrial centres of world socialism and gradually unite with them. Drawn in this way into the path of socialist construction, and bypassing the stages of development when capitalism is the dominant system, they can make rapid economic and cultural progress. Peasant Soviets in the backward ex-colonies, and workers' and peasants' Soviets in the more advanced, will gravitate politically towards the centres of proletarian dictatorship and will in this way be drawn into the general system of the ever-expanding federation of Soviet republics and the world dictatorship of the proletariat.[83]

With the new, terrible defeats of the workers' movement over the following years, this grandiosely optimistic perspective gave way to a defensive position – a minimalist one this time – through a very abrupt political turnaround that was confirmed at the 1935 Seventh Congress. The defence of the Soviet Union came to the fore again, here in the Resolution on the danger of a new world war adopted by the congress (and introduced by Palmiro Togliatti):

> At the present historical juncture, when on one-sixth part of the globe the Soviet Union defends socialism and peace for all humanity, the most vital interests of the workers and toilers of all countries demand that in the struggle against imperialist war before and after the outbreak of hostilities, the defence of the Soviet Union must be considered paramount.[84]

As one might expect, when the Soviet Union was invaded by Nazi Germany the ultimate consequence of this logic was to get rid of the goal of world revolution and the programme of a global USSR, as well as of the Communist International itself. One need only compare the above programmatic statements with Joseph Stalin's explanation of the dissolution of the Comintern in May 1943:

> It facilitates the work of patriots of all countries for uniting all freedom-loving peoples into a single international camp for the fight against the menace of world domination by Hitlerism, thus clearing the way for the future organization of a companionship of nations based upon their equality.[85]

"Cosmopolitanism" as anathema: the Stalinist perversion

Embittered ultranationalisms in interwar Europe naturally considered "cosmopolitanism" a supreme anathema. With the First World War and its exacerbation of nationalist sentiments, nineteenth-century "patriotic" criticism of liberal cosmopolitanism morphed into a heinous assault on the "unpatriotic" political movements and social groups accused of weakening the national bond and held responsible for the defeat in vanquished countries – Germany and Italy in particular. Predictably, the principal targets of this assault were those "cosmopolitans" *par excellence* in the ultranationalist mind: the Marxists and the Jews. What was less predictable was the fact that "cosmopolitanism" would eventually become anathema for Stalinist "Marxism-Leninism" as well, with the same preferred targets – except that "Trotskyites" stood for Marxists, the Stalinists claiming exclusive rights on Marx's legacy.

The genealogy of this mutation deserves consideration. As is well known, Stalin's 1913 *Marxism and the National Question* (initially published as *The Problem of Nationalities and Social Democracy*), a superficial and dogmatic essay on this most complex of questions,[86] was elevated to the status of a major component of the Marxist-Leninist corpus – the paradigmatic elaboration of the Bolshevik theory and programme on the national question – after Stalin prevailed in the power struggle that erupted in Moscow in the wake of Lenin's paralysis and death.

Throughout Stalin's pamphlet, "internationalism" refers only to the pan-Tsarist Russia organisation of the Russian Social-Democratic Labour Party (RSDLP); to the principle, that is, according to which the party strove "to unite locally the workers of all nationalities of Russia into *single, integral* collective bodies, to unite these collective bodies into a *single* party".[87] In defending this principle, Stalin launched a fierce attack on nationalism, putting Great Russian chauvinism on an equal footing with the nationalism that was expanding among oppressed nationalities in the USSR – in a definitely non-Leninist fashion. He probably felt he was entitled to do so, if not obliged, as being a Georgian himself he belonged to one of those oppressed nationalities (in a way that can be compared to the role played by Marx's Jewish origins in his critique of Judaism).

The ultimate antithesis of the RSDLP's "territorial-international" principle was in Stalin's eyes, the General Jewish Labour Union of Lithuania, Poland and Russia, better known as the Bund. This organisation stood for a national-federalist model for the pan-Russian workers' movement, calling for the RSDLP to be turned into a federation of national organisations. Its stance was deemed all the more outrageous by the "internationalists" (with many Jews among them) in that the Bund pretended to organise an ethnic group with no territory of its own, dispersed throughout the *shtetls* of the Pale of Settlement, to the effect that its very character as a nation was disputed.

Thus in 1903 – when the controversy with the Bund reached its peak and when the Jewish organisation broke with the RSDLP – Lenin wrote a polemical article against the Bund in which he tried his best to refute the latter's claim that the Jews constituted a nation.[88] The article manifestly inspired Stalin. Lenin had an easy task demolishing the view that Jews constitute a *worldwide* nation whose only common denominator would be religion, quoting authors from countries such as Austria and France where Jews were "assimilated" to a large extent.[89] Invoking Kautsky's assertion that "language and territory" are the "two principal criteria of a nationality", Lenin then commented: "All that remains for the Bundists is to develop the theory of a separate Russian-Jewish nation, whose language is Yiddish and their territory the Pale of Settlement."[90]

That was in some way an indirect qualification of his own categorical rejection of the Bund's claim: whereas the idea of a "Jewish nation" transcending all borders is indeed a typically Zionist claim, as Lenin emphasised, the Bund's view was actually predicated on the existence of a Yiddish nation (in the Yiddish language, *yidish* means "Jewish").[91] The Bund's reply to the argument that Jews did not have a "language of their own" was precisely that the overwhelming majority of the Jews of the Pale of Settlement spoke Yiddish as their "mother tongue", as stated in a 1904 Bund publication.[92] Lenin himself revised his position afterwards, so much so that he employed the term "Jewish nation" several times in subsequent writings when discussing the Jews of the Pale of Settlement.[93]

The territorial argument with regard to the Jewish nation was used by Otto Bauer in his famous 1907 *The Question of Nationalities and Social Democracy* in a much more nuanced and sophisticated manner than either Kautsky's or Lenin's (not to mention Stalin's).[94] Bauer used it not in order to deny the existence of a Jewish nation in Central Europe – which he acknowledged, rejecting explicitly the idea that territory is an indispensable condition for the existence of a nation – but in order to cast doubt on the possibility of its persistence as a nation in the future.[95] In his pamphlet, Stalin, who of course rejected categorically the very idea of the Jewish nation, referred bizarrely to Bauer in order to vindicate the territorial argument. However, he gave the latter a peculiar twist. Instead of stressing the fact that Jews were not concentrated on a continuous territory where they constitute a majority, this fact became a mere ancillary to the main, dubious argument that only a tiny minority of Jews were peasants and therefore "connected with the land":

> The fact of the matter is primarily that among the Jews there is no large and stable stratum connected with the land, which would naturally rivet the nation together, serving not only as its framework but also as a "national" market. Of the five or six million Russian Jews, only three to four per cent are connected with agriculture in any way. ...

Thus, interspersed as national minorities in areas inhabited by other nationalities, the Jews as a rule serve "foreign" nations as manufacturers and traders and as members of the liberal professions, naturally adapting themselves to the "foreign nations" in respect to language and so forth.[96]

In 1929, at the peak of the ultra-left "Third Period" and at a time when Lenin had been canonised in the Soviet Union and his writings turned into Holy Scripture, Stalin confronted arguments with regard to a statement made by the founder of Bolshevism in 1916. In his theses on "The Socialist Revolution and the Right of Nations to Self-Determination", Lenin had emphasised the necessity of supporting the right of oppressed nations in the Russian empire to free secession, while advocating a federation. The founder of Bolshevism was arguing against those Russian Marxists tempted by the idea of championing a unitary state and restricting the oppressed nations' right to self-determination, or by the idea of postponing the solution to the national question until the achievement of socialism.

Lenin's statement went over the top in his vision of a Jacobin-cosmopolitan future socialist world only in order to better stress, in dialectical fashion, the necessity of recognising the right to self-determination:

The aim of socialism is not only to abolish the present division of mankind into small states and all national isolation; not only to bring the nations closer to each other, but also to merge them. And in order to achieve this aim, we must, on the one hand, explain to the masses the reactionary nature of the ideas of [Karl] Renner and Otto Bauer concerning so-called "cultural national autonomy" and, on the other hand, demand the liberation of the oppressed nations, not only in general, nebulous phrases, not in empty declamations, not by "postponing" the question until socialism is established, but in a clearly and precisely formulated political programme which shall particularly take into account the hypocrisy and cowardice of the Socialists in the oppressing nations. Just as mankind can achieve the abolition of classes only by passing through the transition period of the dictatorship of the oppressed class, so mankind can achieve the inevitable merging of nations only by passing through the transition period of complete liberation of all the oppressed nations, i.e., their freedom to secede.[97]

Stalin's comment in reply to letters that he received on this issue was that it is necessary to distinguish between "bourgeois nations" and "socialist nations". He asserted that Lenin was actually referring to the former, and confirmed that "with the fall of capitalism, such nations must depart from the scene";[98] "socialist nations", however, i.e. Soviet nations, "are arising and developing, and they are far more solidly united than any bourgeois nation."[99] Then, in order to nevertheless reconcile Lenin's statement with his own assertion that "socialist nations" are destined to thrive, Stalin went on to explain that another distinction was needed:

You commit a grave error in putting a sign of equality between the period of the victory of socialism in one country and the period of the victory of socialism on a world scale, in asserting that the disappearance of national differences and national languages, the merging of nations and the formation of one common language, are possible and necessary not only with the victory of socialism on a world scale, but also with the victory of socialism in one country.[100]

"Socialism in one country": this theoretical innovation central to

Stalinism actually laid the ground for a Soviet patriotism, coupled with a *sui generis* internationalism that amounted in fact to the internationalisation of Soviet patriotism. Communist members of "bourgeois nations" had a duty to identify with the thriving "fatherland of socialism". Indeed, their Soviet patriotic duty could very well have taken as its motto "our country, right or wrong!" – as in this August 1927 definition of "internationalism" by Stalin: "He is an internationalist who unreservedly, unhesitatingly and unconditionally is prepared to defend the USSR, because the USSR is the base of the world revolutionary movement, and it is impossible to defend, to advance this revolutionary movement without defending the USSR."[101]

The patriotic mutation was brought to completion after the Soviet Union entered the Second World War, engaging in what the Stalinist regime called the "Great Patriotic War". This went along with the rehabilitation of the Greek Orthodox Church and the resurrection of Slavophilism.[102] "Soviet patriotism" became a highly praised virtue in the Soviet Union and in the world communist movement, while Stalin's brand of "internationalism" reached its logical conclusion in the 1943 dissolution of the Comintern.

Soviet patriotism mutated into full-fledged chauvinism after Moscow emerged victorious from the war, especially when the Soviet Union faced renewed ostracism with the start of the Cold War. It is against this historical background that the campaign against "cosmopolitanism" unfolded. Kolakowski described it in his monumental *Main Currents of Marxism*:

In 1949 the [Soviet] Press launched a campaign against "cosmopolitanism", a vice that was not defined but evidently entailed being anti-patriotic and glorifying the West. As the campaign developed, it was intimated more and more clearly that a cosmopolitan was much the same thing as a Jew. When individuals were pilloried and had previously borne Jewish-sounding names, these were generally mentioned. "Soviet patriotism" was indistinguishable from Russian chauvinism and became an official mania. Propaganda declared incessantly that all important technical inventions and discoveries had been made by Russians, and to mention foreigners in this context was to be guilty of cosmopolitanism and kowtowing to the West.[103]

Isaac Deutscher told the story behind this campaign.[104] The massive demonstrations of sympathy by Russian Jews who, in 1948–49, greeted Golda Meir, the first ambassador to Moscow of the newborn state of Israel, constituted the triggering factor. The Soviet Union had been one of the main sponsors at the United Nations of the new state, to which creation it made a decisive contribution by supplying the Zionist movement with weapons in the first Arab–Israeli war. Nonetheless, Stalin resented this un-authorised public display of support for a foreign state by Soviet citizens, all the more because Israel stunned him with its ingratitude by siding with the West in the Cold War soon after it was born. A crackdown was ordered. "The party agitators began to denounce the state of Israel as a tool of western imperialism; and they upbraided those Soviet Jews who by showing friendliness towards it had shamefully failed to give their undivided loyalty to the Soviet fatherland."[105]

Under the pretext that they had become "assimilated", Soviet Jews were suddenly deprived of many of the rights they had hitherto enjoyed. Jewish theatres, periodicals and publishing houses were closed down, and their personnel purged. Rabbis were arrested and sent to labour camps. Public figures of Jewish origin were persecuted. "The world got an inkling of it from allusions in the Press, which, castigating 'rootless cosmopolitanism' and men of 'uncertain allegiance', revealed systematically the Jewish names of writers who had been known to the public under Russian pseudonyms."[106]

A revealing example of the anti-cosmopolitan campaign is an article signed F. Chernov and published in March 1949 in *Bolshevik*, the theoretical and political magazine of the Central Committee of the All-Union Communist Party (Bolsheviks) – as the ruling party was called until 1952, when it became the Communist Party of the Soviet Union (CPSU). The article was entitled: "Bourgeois Cosmopolitanism and its Reactionary Role".[107] It begins by reporting that Soviet newspapers "unmasked an unpatriotic group of theatre critics, of rootless cosmopolitans, who came out against Soviet patriotism, against the great cultural achievements of the Russian people and of other peoples in our country".[108] Several pages of anti-cosmopolitan rant follow, with many quotes from Stalin and a few others ranging from Marx to Zhdanov. Here are two excerpts:

Cosmopolitanism is the negation of patriotism, its opposite. It advocates absolute apathy towards the fate of the Motherland. Cosmopolitanism denies the existence of any moral or civil obligations of people to their nation and Motherland. ...

Present-day bourgeois cosmopolitanism with its call for the repudiation of national sovereignty, with its notions of "one-world government," the creation of the "United States of Europe," etc. is an ideological "basis" and "consecration" of the assembling under the aegis of American imperialism of a "union of imperialists" in the name of the struggle against the toiling masses, against the Soviet Union and people's democracies, against the irresistible growth over the entire world of the forces of socialism and democracy.[109]

The party unmasked the antipatriotic, bourgeois-cosmopolitan essence of servility before the capitalist West. It revealed that this cringing before foreign countries inevitably leads to national treason and to betrayal of the interests of the Soviet people and the socialist Fatherland. The unmasking of antipatriotic groups of bourgeois cosmopolitans, the struggle against the ideology of bourgeois cosmopolitanism, is a striking expression of the concern of the Bolshevik Party about the education of the toiling masses of our country in the spirit of life-giving, Soviet patriotism.[110]

The campaign was stopped after Stalin's death. Kolakowski's description of the way the end to the campaign was signalled – through the "special code" to which readers of Soviet newspapers were accustomed – is worth quoting:

On the face of things it might seem that "Let us fight against cosmopolitanism and nationalism" was the same as "Let us fight against nationalism and cosmopolitanism"; but as soon as the Soviet reader came across the latter formulation after Stalin's death he realized that "the line had changed" and that nationalism was now the principal enemy.[111]

With the start of "de-Stalinisation" in Khrushchev's Soviet Union, the eyes of many Communists were opened; more accurately, their mouths were opened, as it is difficult to believe that they had not been aware of the realities they denounced when the green light finally came from Moscow. A striking example is one of the most prominent historical figures of American communism, the well-known writer Howard Fast – himself of Jewish background – who was awarded the Stalin Peace Prize in 1954. The 26 April 1956 issue of *The Daily Worker*, the newspaper of the Communist

Party USA, carried an article by Fast entitled "Cosmopolitanism". Its first paragraphs are symptomatic:

> At this writing, no explanation has been forthcoming from the Soviet Union that would enable us to place the destruction of Jewish culture there in some sort of perspective. I do not mean that it can ever be written away; the dead remain dead, and the immensity of the acknowledged injustice can only be atoned for by a bitter memory that pledges itself that under socialism this can never happen again. ...
>
> You will remember, perhaps, that some of the broadest and most vituperative attacks against critics and writers – the great majority of them Jewish – were rationalized under a theory called "cosmopolitanism." This name was given to the elaboration of the "sins" for which the writers were condemned, and the "theory of cosmopolitanism" was developed to characterize what the theorizers designated as an evil trend in working class culture. ...
>
> Insofar as I know or have been able to learn, Marx, Engels and Lenin appear to have been quite unaware of such a trend or even the possibility of such a trend. If anything, these three men put forth the concept of a movement dedicated to proletarian internationalism, a movement that specified the working class as a world phenomenon – and looked forward to a time when mankind would unite in a brotherhood that transcends all national boundaries.[112]

Cosmopolitanism and "globalisation"

With the end of the Stalinist campaign, "cosmopolitanism" faded away as a major issue in Communist circles, as well as in the public debate in general. It remained, however, in substance if not in terminology, a key concern of thinkers like Karl Jaspers or Hannah Arendt in their reflection on the lessons of the historical catastrophes that struck the world during the first half of the twentieth century. A radical thinker and an admirer of Rosa Luxemburg, Arendt's views on cosmopolitanism are here of particular interest.

While she adhered undoubtedly to a cosmopolitan conception of humanness, harshly critical of any kind of ethno-nationalism including the Jewish version, Arendt tried to strike a balance between the universal and the particular and produced what Natan Sznaider called "rooted cosmopolitanism", defined as "universal values that descend from the level of abstract philosophy and are emotionally engaging … in people's everyday lives."[113] More original still with regard to her intellectual profile is her negative appraisal of institutional cosmopolitanism *stricto sensu* as she expressed it in discussing the German philosopher Karl Jaspers. Contrarily to Kant's view, Arendt could not even conceive of a *civitas gentium*, whether federal or not, that would not be a global Leviathan:

> Nobody can be a citizen of the world as he is a citizen of his country. … No matter what form a world government with centralized power over the whole globe might assume, the very notion of one sovereign force ruling the whole earth, holding the monopoly of all means of violence, unchecked and uncontrolled by other sovereign powers, is not only a forbidding nightmare of tyranny, it would be the end of all political life as we know it. … The establishment of one sovereign world state, far from being the prerequisite for world citizenship, would be the end of all citizenship. It would not be the climax of world politics, but quite literally its end.[114]

This view, in all likelihood, is what explains Arendt's rejection of the idea of an international criminal court, as she expressed it in the 1964 postscript to her *Eichmann in Jerusalem* (a rejection that Seyla Benhabib found "baffling"[115]): "It is quite conceivable that certain political responsibilities among nations might some day be adjudicated in an international court; what is inconceivable is that such a court would be a criminal tribunal which pronounces on the guilt or innocence of individuals."[116]

Arendt's pessimistic view, more pessimistic than Kant's, precludes, yet, the possibility of utopia, what Ernst Bloch called "the principle of hope". Writing in the same period under the strain of the Second World War followed by the Cold War, Bloch, speaking of Kant, acknowledged that

> This pessimism differs at least from the trustfulness of those pacifists who saw peace and not the armaments industry promoted in an American "world-republic". … This kind of thing in fact can only befall the "defence community" of wolves, the pacifism of deception, the same deception which lyingly changes the victim of aggression into the aggressor and manufactures atom bombs for the salvation of civilization.[117]

The problem, as Bloch noted it, is that "pacifism almost possesses the tradition of a *separate utopia*. A utopia which, though it is also occasionally contained in the social ones, still by no means coincides with them."[118] However,

> the ancient dream of peace presupposes almost even more cogently than any other element of social utopia clear supports and correction. … The swords will only certainly become ploughshares when the soil over which the plough passes belongs to all; not an hour earlier, nor an hour later. Capitalist

peace is a paradox which spreads fear more than ever and which enjoins the nations to defend the cause of peace to the utmost, most strenuously; whereas socialist peace is a tautology.[119]

Predictably, "cosmopolitanism" has gained new currency in intellectual discourse since the early 1990s, more so than during any previous epoch in history, with the advent of the new era in the history of world capitalist development that has been labelled "globalisation" – an era that started with the confluence in the 1980s of the "Information Age" and the worldwide neoliberal offensive, accelerating considerably the international circulation of capital and goods, and was marked by the end of world "bipolarity" as a result of the downfall of the Soviet Union and the Stalinist system of East-European states.[120]

The most visible manifestation of the new trend – because it pertains to the dominant class ideology of the "globalisation" era – is what Peter Gowan, its sharpest Marxist critic, called "new liberal cosmopolitanism":[121]

> Viewed historically, the new doctrine is a radicalization of the Anglo-American tradition that has conceived itself as upholding a liberal internationalism, based on visions of a single human race peacefully united by free trade and common legal norms, led by states featuring civic liberties and representative institutions. ...
>
> The new liberal cosmopolitanism, by contrast, seeks to overcome the limits of national sovereignty by constructing a global order that will govern important political as well as economic aspects of both the internal and external behaviour of states. This is not a conception advocating any world government empowered to decide the great international issues of the day. Rather, it proposes a set of disciplinary

regimes – characteristically dubbed, in the oleaginous jargon of the period, "global governance" – reaching deep into the economic, social and political life of the states subject to it, while safeguarding international flows of finance and trade.[122]

Gowan took care, however, to distinguish this "new liberal cosmopolitanism" from "the more democratic cosmopolitanism" upheld by several authors. Among the latter, as Nadia Urbinati explained,[123] a further distinction can be made between "cosmopolitan democracy" as conceptualised principally by Jürgen Habermas on the philosophical plane[124] and its "cosmopolitical" implementation as advocated chiefly by Daniele Archibugi and David Held on the institutional level.[125] To the extent that a neo-Kantian rights-based approach of cosmopolitanism is central to this doctrine of democratic cosmopolitanism, there is already a clear difference between the range of human rights that its upholders are mostly concerned with, i.e. the conventional rights, and the range of rights that chiefly preoccupy legal thinkers, such as Boaventura de Sousa Santos, who seek a "cosmopolitan legality" from the standpoint of the forces active in the World Social Forum.[126]

The question of immigration is a good touchstone of the difference: whereas advocates of "cosmopolitan democracy" support the integration of immigrants as citizens – thus converging with the enlightened section of the mainstream – radical thinkers such as Etienne Balibar, Marie-Claire Caloz-Tschopp and Sandro Mezzadra[127] defend the right of the global poor to circulation, immigration and settlement, in a way that far exceeds the limits of bourgeois admissibility.

The key problem with "cosmopolitan democracy", however, resides in its institutional views. Essentially, upholders of the doctrine advocate the extension and development of intergovernmental institutions with an enhanced role for both non-governmental organisations ("civil society") and democratically elected representatives within them and beside them, acting as conveyor belts of the global "public sphere"; this development of global governance would go along with a shrinkage of state sovereignty. The main deficiency of this doctrine comes most clearly in sight through Archibugi's own acknowledgement of its aporia:

> There is undoubtedly a contradiction here: the cosmopolitical project would delegate to structures devoid of coercive powers (international judicial bodies, institutions of the world's citizens) the job of establishing when force should be used, while asking states, who monopolize the means of military might to acquiesce in their decisions. But if the governments that defined themselves as 'enlightened' during the Gulf and Kosovo wars intend to perform their democratic mandate effectively, they should consult global civil society and international judicial authorities before flexing their muscles.[128]

From a Marxist point of view, a plain "realist" one, or even one based on common sense, it is obvious that the "if" of the last sentence can only be seen as self-delusion or wishful thinking – when not as an expression of "the class consciousness of frequent travellers", to put it in Craig Calhoun's ironic phrase. Calhoun observes that "advocates of cosmopolitan democracy often offer a vision of political reform attractive to élites because it promises to find virtue without radical redistribution of wealth or power."[129] Whereas, as Gowan emphasised,

> Any prospect of bringing humanity towards genuine unity on a global scale would have to confront the social and economic

relations of actually existing capitalism with a clarity and trenchancy from which most representatives of this current shrink; and any hope of altering these can only be nullified by evasion or edulcoration of the realities of the sole superpower.[130]

Archibugi seems to endorse this judgement when he writes in the concluding sentence of a reply to his critics: "Cosmopolitan democracy will be nothing more than a miserable consolation if it proves incapable of restraining the consolidation of this increasingly hegemonic power."[131] "Cosmopolitan democracy" views have also been criticised on the left from a perspective questioning "the cogency and desirability of making the cosmos into a unified political space"[132] – in terms reminiscent of Arendt's opposition quoted above. Hence Timothy Brennan's defence of sovereignty:

> We need to be very cautious in contemplating any cosmopolis that would short-circuit the existing nation-states in the name of the people: on that imaginary terrain, too many powerful interests are already entrenched. ... We should be encouraging popular efforts in Southern Mexico, Colombia, Indonesia or Palestine – and so many other parts of the world – to establish a modicum of real sovereignty, rather than constructing intricate theoretical edifices liable to weaken the very ability to imagine it. That does not clash with the need for new forms of cross-border mobilization, radical cultural combination, international campaigns for civic solidarity and labour protection.[133]

Here again, this kind of critique of "cosmopolitanism" risks precluding the indispensable driving force of utopia: instead of being connected in an indissociable manner with the socialist dream, as Bloch advocated, the aspiration to a peaceful, unified humanity is replaced with the defence of national sovereignty. No wonder, then, that Brennan resorts to the outworn artifice of opposing "cosmopolitanism" to "internationalism", which is always metamorphosed in such instances into "inter-nationalism". True, he regards "the existing nation-state system" as "a transitional arena", but adds that "for the moment [it] contains the only structures through which transnational forms of solidarity might emerge in the only way they can – slowly and for many generations."[134]

This sounds like a reinstatement of *The Communist Manifesto*'s elementary acknowledgement that the immediate arena of the class struggle is the nation – with the difference that in the *Manifesto* this went along with a cosmopolitan perspective as well as with a revolutionary prospect that sharply contrasts with the "slowness" that is ascribed here not to the socialist transformation, but to the mere emergence of transnational forms of solidarity (which have actually existed in different forms for several generations).

Although the defence of national sovereignty is certainly warranted and necessary in the face of imperialist coercion, it appears inevitably anachronistic, and is so indeed when turned into an unsurpassable horizon of our epoch, at a time when "globalisation" is certainly a reality and not an empty catch-phrase, and an irreversible reality at that (unless one contemplates its reversal through an historical regression that could only be produced by a catastrophe of immense proportions).

There should be no contradiction but rather indispensable complementarity between the national level and the international-cosmopolitan one in the struggle for social rights, if properly understood. This goes also for the struggle of "postcolonial nationalism" itself. When Pheng Cheah characterises "contemporary transnational activity aimed at postcolonial transformation as aporetic cases of postcolonial nationalism in a cosmopolitical force field",[135] he wrongly postulates the aporia as immanent in the apparently logical opposition between the national and the cosmopolitan. As we have seen, this opposition is valid only if by nationalism one means exclusive ultra-nationalism – a brand that is much more inherent in the nationalism of imperialist countries than in that of postcolonial countries – and/or if by cosmopolitanism one means a veiled attempt to impose the will and culture of one state or a group of states on the rest of the world.

But cosmopolitanism is of various kinds, like nationalism. It is not necessarily imperialism in disguise, even when expressed from the heart of the sole superpower. The American philosopher Martha Nussbaum, one of the foremost proponents of moral/philosophical cosmopolitanism à la Diogenes, actually clashed with American patriotism and exceptionalism.[136] Moreover, Francis Fukuyama himself, one of the foremost doctrinaires of US imperialism, derided her cosmopolitanism as having "no emotional appeal to anyone except a small group of intellectuals like the author herself, and perhaps a stratum of CEOs of multinationals for whom she presumably has little sympathy."[137] Provided it is well understood, it is in fact internationalist cosmopolitanism much more than postcolonial nationalism that is the true antithesis of neoliberal cosmopolitanism. As Daniele Conversi aptly put it:

> Clearly, there is no single cosmopolitan vision, but a plurality of competing cosmopolitan projects. A convincing cosmopolitan agenda can only be pursued by encompassing the human variety of local, national and universal ideals, making them compatible, rather than competitive (or mutually exclusive). And, if the only feasible rational goal is human coexistence (rather than destructive processes such as domination, hegemony, obliteration or assimilation), then cosmopolitanism

can only be conceived as incompatible with homogenization and indeed with contemporary globalization.[138]

National emancipation movements in postcolonial countries can fit perfectly in the cosmopolitan struggle for global transformation as necessary moments of this struggle, as components of the global struggle: this view was best theorised by Lenin a long time ago, and has been implemented countless times in contemporary history, most recently and clearly by the new left-wing popular movements in Latin America. While fighting for the defence and expansion of national-based social gains, most working-class organisations and other social movements already fight for their international extension and institutionalisation, in the knowledge that this is the surest way to consolidate them and prevent the exploiters from undermining whatever gains there are by bringing international competition into play.[139]

The confluence of all these fights and others lies at the heart of the World Social Forum as the "most accomplished manifestation" of what Boaventura de Sousa Santos calls "insurgent cosmopolitanism", defined as follows:

> It consists of the transnationally organized resistance against the unequal exchanges produced or intensified by globalized localisms and localized globalisms. This resistance is organized through local/global linkages between social organizations and movements representing those classes and social groups victimized by hegemonic globalization and united in concrete struggles against exclusion, subordinate inclusion, destruction of livelihoods and ecological destruction, political oppression, or cultural suppression, etc. They take advantage of the possibilities of transnational interaction created by the world system in transition, including those resulting from the

revolution in information technology and communications and from the reduction of travel costs. Insurgent cosmopolitan activities include, among many others: egalitarian transnational North- South and South-South networks of solidarity among social movements and progressive NGOs; the new working-class internationalism (dialogues between workers' organizations in different regional blocs); transnational coalitions among workers of the same multinational corporation operating in different countries; coalitions of workers and citizenship groups in the struggle against sweatshops, discriminatory labor practices and slave labor; international networks of alternative legal aid; transnational human rights organizations; worldwide networks of feminist, indigenous, ecological or alternative development movements and associations; and literary, artistic and scientific movements on the periphery of the world system in search of alternative non-imperialist, counter-hegemonic cultural values, involved in studies using post-colonial or minority perspectives.[140]

Boaventura de Sousa Santos concludes his article thus: "From now on, what we call global and globalization cannot but be conceived of as the provisory, partial and reversible result of a permanent struggle between two modes of production of globalization, indeed, between two globalizations."[141] This is, indeed, why the organisers of the World Social Forum insisted on replacing the label "anti-globalist" that the media stuck on them with "alter-globalist".

The socialist struggle must aspire to superseding the cosmopolitan accomplishment of capitalism on the basis of global justice: it would be inconsistent with the very nature of the socialist project to oppose globalisation *per se*, in a Luddite-like manner, and long for national retrenchment, thus seeking to "roll back the wheel of history".[142] The final sentences of Bloch's *The Principle of*

Hope summarise aptly and nicely what lies at the heart of Marx's world-historical vision, and should remain at the core of any reflection that takes Marx as its principal inspiration:

> Marx describes as his final concern "the development of the wealth of human nature"; this *human* wealth as well as that of *nature* as a whole lies solely in the tendency-latency in which the world finds itself – *vis-à-vis de tout*. This glance therefore confirms that man everywhere is still living in prehistory, indeed all and everything still stands before the creation of a world, of a right world. *True genesis is not at the beginning but at the end,* and it starts to begin only when society and existence become radical, i.e. grasp their roots. But the root of history is the working, creating human being who reshapes and overhauls the given facts. Once he has grasped himself and established what is his, without expropriation and alienation, in real democracy, there arises in the world something which shines into the childhood of all and in which no one has yet been: homeland.[143]

Notes

1   For good synthetic overviews of the history of the concept, see H. J. Busch and A. Horstmann, "Kosmopolit, Kosmopolitismus. 1." in Joachim Ritter, Karlfried Gründer and Gottfried Gabriel, eds, *Historisches Wörterbuch der Philosophie* (HWPh), vol. 4, Basel: Schwabe Verlag, 1976, pp. 1155–8, and Pauline Kleingeld and Eric Brown, "Cosmopolitanism", in Edward N. Zalta, ed., *The Stanford Encyclopedia of Philosophy*, Winter 2006 Edition; http://plato.stanford.edu/archives/win2006/entries/cosmopolitanism/

2   According to Diogenes Laertius in his *The Lives and Opinions of Eminent Philosophers*, Book VI, "Life of Diogenes", 6 (trans. C. D. Yonge, 1853): http://classicpersuasion.org/pw/diogenes/

3   Dante Alighieri, *De Monarchia* (trans. Aurelia Henry, 1904): http://oll.libertyfund.org/index.php?option=com_staticxt&staticfile=show.php%3Ftitle=2196&Itemid=27

4   Anacharsis Cloots, *La république universelle ou Adresse aux tyrannicides*, 1792

(original French text available on the Internet from various websites). On the cosmopolitan views of Cloots, see Alexander Bevilacqua, "Conceiving the Republic of Mankind: The Political Thought of Anacharsis Cloots", *History of European Ideas*, vol. 38, no. 4, December 2012, pp. 550–69. See also Catherine Lu, "World Government", in Edward N. Zalta, ed., *The Stanford Encyclopedia of Philosophy*, Fall 2008 Edition: http://plato.stanford.edu/archives/fall2008/entries/world-government/, as well as the above-quoted entry on "Cosmopolitanism".

5   Immanuel Kant, *Perpetual Peace: A Philosophical Sketch* (different translations available on the Internet from various websites; here: www.mtholyoke.edu/acad/intrel/kant/kant1.htm)

6   The subtitle of Kant's Third Article is "The Law of World Citizenship Shall Be Limited to Conditions of Universal Hospitality".

7   "The spirit of commerce, which is incompatible with war, sooner or later gains the upper hand in every state. As the power of money is perhaps the most dependable of all the powers (means) included under the state power, states see themselves forced, without any moral urge, to promote honourable peace and by mediation to prevent war wherever it threatens to break out." Kant, *Perpetual Peace*: www.mtholyoke.edu/acad/intrel/kant/firstsup.htm

8   "Republicanism" is restricted by Kant to the English model of separation of powers and representative government as theorised by Locke and Montesquieu (with an explicit rejection of Rousseau's direct democracy). This model is best embodied, according to Kant, in constitutional monarchy, with the key condition that war should be approved by the people's representatives.

9   Kant cited Adam Smith's *The Wealth of Nations* in his 1797 *The Metaphysics of Morals*, trans. and ed. by Mary Gregor, Cambridge: Cambridge University Press, 1996, p. 71.

10 Adam Smith, *An Inquiry into the Nature and Causes of the Wealth of Nations* (available on the Internet from various websites), Book V, Ch. 2, Art. 2 (emphasis added). A similar statement, with the term "capital", appears at the end of Book III: "A merchant, it has been said very properly, is not necessarily the citizen of any particular country. It is in a great measure indifferent to him from what place he carries on his trade; and a very trifling disgust will make him remove his capital, and together with it all the industry which it supports, from one country to another."

11 Friedrich List, *The National System of Political Economy*, trans. Sampson Lloyd, 1909; available on the Internet from various websites.

12 The adjective *bodenloser* has been mistranslated by Sampson Lloyd as "bottomless" in the preface, "boundless" in ch. 15 and "unfathomable" in ch. 33 of the standard English edition.

13 List, *The National System of Political Economy*, beginning of Book II, ch. 15, § 1. Sampson Lloyd translated *"bodenlosem Kosmopolitismus"* here as "boundless cosmopolitanism".

14 John Stuart Mill, *Principles of Political Economy with Some of Their Applications to Social Philosophy* (available on the Internet from various websites), Book III, Ch. XVII, III.17.3.

15 Ibid.

16 Karl Marx, *Contribution to the Critique of Hegel's Philosophy of Law. Introduction* (hereafter *Critique of Hegel. Introduction*), MECW, vol. 3, p. 175.

17 Roman Rosdolsky's "The *Neue Rheinische Zeitung* and the Jews", appendix to *Engels and the "Nonhistoric" Peoples: The National Question in the Revolution of 1848* (trans. and ed. by John-Paul Himka, *Critique: Journal of Socialist Theory*, vol. 18, no. 1, 1991, pp. 191–207) is a very useful introduction to reading Karl Marx's *On the Jewish Question*, MECW, vol. 3, pp. 146–74, situating it in context.

18 See on this, among others, Daniel Bensaïd's comment on Marx's pamphlet in Karl Marx, *Sur la Question Juive. Présentation et commentaires de Daniel Bensaïd*, Paris: Textuel, 2006.

19 Marx, *On the Jewish Question*, pp. 170, 172.

20 In German, "citizenship" is linked to the term and concept of "state" [*Staatsbürgerschaft*], whereas in other European languages it is rooted in the Latin *civitas* – itself an equivalent of the Greek *polis*.

21 Members of the First International used to call each other "citizen", not "comrade", which later became used in the Second International.

22 Marx, *On the Jewish Question*, pp. 162, 164.

23 Marx, *Critique of Hegel. Introduction*, p. 186.

24 Ibid., p. 187.

25 Ibid., p. 176.

26 Karl Marx, *A Contribution to the Critique of Political Economy. Preface*, MECW, vol. 29, p. 264. The translation of "*geniale Skizze*" as "brilliant essay" in the MECW weakens the expression.

27 Frederick Engels, *Outlines of a Critique of Political Economy*, MECW, vol. 3, p. 422.

28 "This is why modern liberal economics cannot comprehend the restoration of the mercantile system by List, whilst for us the matter is quite simple. The inconsistency and ambiguity of liberal economics must of necessity dissolve again into its basic components. Just as theology must either regress to blind faith or progress towards free philosophy, free trade must produce the restoration of monopolies on the one hand and the abolition of private property on the other. The only *positive* advance which liberal economics has made is the elaboration of the laws of private property." Ibid., p. 421.

29 See Frederick Engels (F. Oswald), "*Ernst Moritz Arndt*" (*Telegraph für Deutschland*, no. 2–5, January 1841), MECW, vol. 2, pp. 137–50.

30 Engels, *Outlines*, pp. 419–20.

31 Ibid., p. 423.

32 Ibid., p. 420.

33 Karl Marx, *Economic and Philosophic Manuscripts of 1844*, MECW, vol. 3, p. 291.

34 Karl Marx, "Draft of an Article on Friedrich List's book: *Das Nationale System der Politischen Oekonomie*", MECW, vol. 4, p. 280.

35 Karl Marx and Frederick Engels, *The German Ideology*, MECW, vol. 5, p. 57.

36 Ibid., p. 159.

37 Ibid., p. 194.

38 Ibid., p. 470.

39 Ibid., p. 88.

40 Ibid., pp. 48–9. The last sentence is from Marx and Engels' joint manuscript.

41 Frederick Engels, "The Festival of Nations in London", MECW, vol. 6, p. 3.

42 Ibid., pp. 7–8.

43 Frederick Engels, "Reform Movement in France – Banquet of Dijon" (*Northern Star*, 18 December 1847), MECW, vol. 6, p. 399. The criticism of French chauvinism is a recurrent theme in Marx and Engels' writings.

44 Karl Marx and Frederick Engels, *Manifesto of the Communist Party*, MECW, vol. 6, p. 488.

45 Karl Marx, "Speech on the Question of Free Trade", MECW, vol. 6, p. 464.

46 On the evolution of Engels' prognosis of revolution, see my "Engels: theorist of war, theorist of revolution", *International Socialism*, no. 97, Winter 2002, pp. 69-89; also available at: http://pubs.socialistreviewindex.org.uk/isj97/achcar.htm

47 Engels replaced "the national class" (*nationalen Klasse*) with "the leading class of the nation", for the sake of clarity, in the 1888 English edition of the *Manifesto*.

48 Marx and Engels, *Manifesto of the Communist Party*, pp. 502–3. The best discussion of this passage is Roman Rosdolsky, "The Workers and the Fatherland: A Note on a Passage in the *Communist Manifesto*", *Science and Society*, vol. 29, no. 3, 1965, pp. 330–7; available on the Internet at: www.marxists.org/archive/rosdolsky/1965/workers.htm

49 Frederick Engels, "Rapid Progress of Communism in Germany" (*The New Moral World*, no. 25, 13 December 1844), MECW, vol. 4, p. 232. According to Franz Mehring, Marx "assisted at the birth" of this poem as well as the famous *Deutschland. Ein Wintermärchen* and others of Heine's political satires (Franz Mehring, *Karl Marx: The Story of His Life*, trans. Edward Fizgerald, ch. 3, § 5 (available on the Internet at: www.marxists.org/archive/mehring/1918/marx/index.htm). On the importance of the Silesian uprising in Marx's political education, see in particular Michael Löwy, *The Theory of Revolution in the Young Marx* (Leiden: Brill, 2003; repr. Chicago: Haymarket, 2005). On Heine's political thought and his influence on Marx, see in particular Stathis Kouvelakis, *Philosophy and Revolution: From Kant to Marx,* trans. G. M. Goshgarian, London: Verso, 2003.

50 Rosdolsky himself omits any mention of it in "The Workers and the Fatherland".

51 Marx and Engels, *Manifesto of the Communist Party*, p. 497.

52 Pheng Cheah, "Cosmopolitanism", *Theory, Culture & Society*, vol. 23, no. 2–3, 2006, p. 490.

53 Marx, *The Eighteenth Brumaire of Louis Bonaparte*, MECW, vol. 11, p. 192.

54 Marx, "Second Address of the General Council of the International Workingmen's Association on the Franco–Prussian War", MECW, vol. 22, p. 268.

55 Ibid., footnote a. The translation of the original *Vaterland* as "native country" in the MECW has been corrected here.

56 Ibid.

57 Karl Marx, *Grundrisse*, MECW, vol. 28, p. 10.

58 Marx, *Contribution to the Critique of Political Economy*, p. 384.

59 Marx, *The Civil War in France. Address of the General Council of the International Working Men's Association*, MECW, vol. 22, p. 354.

60 Karl Marx and Frederick Engels, *The Alliance of Socialist Democracy and the International Working Men's Association*, MECW, Vol. 23, p. 560.

61 Ibid., p. 554. In the English translation published in the MECW, "*cosmopolite*" has

been turned into "worldwide". French original: A.I.T., *L'Alliance de la Démocratie Socialiste et l'Association Internationale des Travailleurs. Rapport et documents publiés par ordre du Congrès International de la Haye*, London: A. Darson, 1873, p. 103.

62 "Frederick Engels to Friedrich Adolph Sorge", (12 [–17] Sept. 1874), MECW, vol. 45, p. 41.

63 Karl Marx and Frederick Engels, "For Poland", MECW, vol. 24, p. 57.

64 Karl Marx, "First Address of the General Council of the International Working Men's Association on the Franco–Prussian War", MECW, vol. 22, p. 7.

65 Karl Marx, *Marginal Notes on the Programme of the German Workers' Party*, MECW, vol. 24, pp. 89–90.

66 For a typology/chronology of workers' international organisations, see Marcel Van der Linden, "Labour Internationalism", in idem., *Workers of the World: Essays Toward a Global Labor History*, Leiden: Brill, 2008, pp. 259-283.

67 Engels, *Anti-Dühring: Herr Eugen Dühring's Revolution in Science*, MECW, vol. 25, p. 305.

68 Karl Kautsky, *Foundations of Christianity* [1908] (trans. Henry Mins, MIA (www.marxists.org/archive/kautsky/1908/christ/index.htm), Book Three, Chapter II.

69 Theodor Mommsen, *The History of Rome* [1856] (trans. William Purdie Dickson, available on the Internet at: www.gutenberg.org/ebooks/10706), Book Fifth, Chapter 11.

70 Karl Kautsky, *Thomas More and his Utopia* (trans. Henry James Stenning, available on the Internet at: www.marxists.org/archive/kautsky/1888/more/index.htm), Part 1, Chapter 1.3. There is a similar and more extensive use of the attribute "cosmopolitan" applied to the Christian religion in Paul Lafargue, *Le déterminisme économique de Karl Marx. Recherches sur l'origine et l'évolution des idées de Justice, du Bien, de l'Âme et de Dieu* [1909] (available on the website *Gallica/BNF*, at: http://gallica.bnf.fr/ark:/12148/bpt6k80118z.r=lafargue.langEN)

71 Antonio Gramsci, *Prison Notebooks* (ed. and trans. by Joseph A. Buttigieg, with Antonio Callari for vol. I, New York: Columbia University Press, 1992, 1996, 2007). This translation is incomplete: it includes only eight of Gramsci's eleven major notebooks (out of a total of twenty-nine). Most of the occurrences of the term and its derivatives in Gramsci's *Prison Notebooks* are indicated in the Thematic Index (*Indice per argomenti*) of the Italian edition, the Istituto Gramsci's *edizione critica*. They are listed in the fourth and last volume under *"cosmopolitismo"* and *"intellettuali: carattere cosmopolita degli –"*: Antonio Gramsci, *Quaderni del carcere, Edizione critica dell'Istituto Gramsci*, 2nd edn, Turin: Einaudi, 1977, vol. 4, pp. 3181, 3210. On "cosmopolitanism" in Gramsci's work, see the essays collected in Maria Proto, ed., *Gramsci e l'Internazionalismo*, Manduria-Bari-Roma: Piero Lacaita Editore, 1967.

72 In reviewing an article that he found "mediocre", written by a pro-British Afghan diplomat on new evolutions within Islam, Gramsci makes an interesting point – albeit very questionable when turned into a general rule – about the contrast between "theocratic cosmopolitanism" and the "national sentiment" of religious heresies:

"Christianity has taken nine centuries to evolve and to adapt, and it has done so in small steps, etc.: Islam is forced into a headlong rush. But, in fact, it reacts just like

Christianity: the great heresy from which the real heresies will arise is the 'national sentiment' against theocratic cosmopolitanism. Then the theme of a return to 'origins' will arise in exactly the same way as in Christianity, a return to the purity of the earliest religious texts as opposed to the corruption of the official hierarchy – this is exactly what the Wahhabis stand for …" (Gramsci, *Prison Notebooks*, vol. I, Notebook 2, § 90, pp. 333–4.)

The fact is that history has seen several instances where heresies of a fundamentalist or "return-to-origin" character upheld the original universalist message of their religion against its nationalisation by the powers that be. Thus Wahhabism, for instance, could be equally seen in the late nineteenth century as waging an Arab-nationalist struggle against the Ottomans, or a pan-Islamist one against the increasing nationalism ("Turkification") of the latter, or else a combination of both. Besides, Gramsci's linguistic-based parallel between "Catholic cosmopolitanism" in medieval Central and Western Europe and what he called the "cosmopolitan" unity of the Chinese in confronting European and Japanese imperialisms is rather unconvincing (Ibid., vol. II, Notebook 5, § 23, p. 286).

73 Gramsci, *Quaderni del carcere*, Notebook 9, § 127, p. 1190. This text was written in 1932. Alberto Toscano kindly checked my translation of the Italian original.

74 Jane Degras, ed., *The Communist International 1919–1943: Documents*, vol. I, London: Oxford University Press, 1956, p. 19.

75 Ibid., p. 35.

76 Ibid., p. 53.

77 Ibid., p. 163.

78 Jane Degras, ed., *The Communist International 1919–1943: Documents*, vol. II, London: Oxford University Press, 1960, p. 23.

79 Ibid., p. 113.

80 Ibid., p. 117.

81 Ibid., p. 325.

82 Ibid., p. 465.

83 Ibid., p. 508.

84 Jane Degras, ed., *The Communist International 1919–1943: Documents*, vol. III, London: Oxford University Press, 1965, p. 378.

85 Ibid., p. 476.

86 For a concise but nevertheless thorough critique of Stalin's pamphlet and its differences with Lenin's writings on the national question, see Michael Löwy, "Le problème de l'histoire: Remarques de théorie et de méthode", in Georges Haupt, Michael Löwy and Claudie Weill, *Les marxistes et la question nationale*, Paris: François Maspero, 1974, pp. 386–8.

87 Joseph Stalin, *Marxism and the National Question* [1913] (MIA, www.marxists. org/reference/archive/stalin/works/1913/03a.htm), Chapter VII: "The National Question in Russia."

88 Vladimir I. Lenin, "The Position of the Bund in the Party" [1903] (MIA, www. marxists.org/archive/lenin/works/1903/oct/22a.htm).

89 The two books by Shlomo Sand – *The Invention of the Jewish People*, trans. Yael Lotan, London: Verso, 2009, and *The Invention of the Land of Israel: From Holy Land to Homeland*, trans. Geremy Forman, London: Verso, 2012 – that were

published after the first writing of this essay are an important contribution to that debate.

90 Nathan Weinstock – in *Le pain de misère. Histoire du mouvement ouvrier juif en Europe*, vol. I: *L'empire russe jusqu'en 1914*, Paris: La Découverte, 1984, p. 194 – points to the fact that the Soviet Union actually implemented this very programme in the 1920s through national Yiddish-speaking soviets.

91 "We have forgotten that Yiddish-speaking Jews were no mere religious or linguistic minority but formed one of Europe's nations, ultimately more populous than many others ... The Yiddish people must be counted among the founder nations of Europe." Paul Kriwaczek, *Yiddish Civilisation: The Rise and Fall of a Forgotten Nation*, New York: Vintage Books, 2006, pp. 5–6.

92 Quoted in ibid., p. 295.

93 See Weinstock, *Le pain de misère*, vol. I, pp. 193–5.

94 Otto Bauer, *The Question of Nationalities and Social Democracy*, trans. Joseph O'Donnell, Minneapolis: University of Minnesota Press, 2000. See, in particular, in ch. 4, the section entitled "National Autonomy for the Jews?", pp. 291–308.

95 "It is generally incorrect to claim that a geographically defined territory is the precondition for the preservation of a nation. The history of the Jews, who for so many centuries have claimed the status of a nation without possessing their own territory, discredits this opinion. However, we now know how this was possible. The Jews, as representatives of the monetary economy in a world based on the natural economy, although they lived in the midst of European peoples, maintained such a loose interactive community with these peoples that they were able to preserve their own cultural community. Capitalist society, which everywhere destroys the old natural economy and, through capitalist commodity production, makes the monetary economy generally constitutive of society – and, in the process, as Marx says, makes the Christians into Jews – also make the Jews into Christians. Territory is not the condition of national being insofar as the community of domicile is still not the same as the community of interaction. However, the moment the Jews and the Christians no longer embody different economic principles and must all act as organs of the same economic system – the capitalist mode of production – the community of domicile produces such an intimate community of interaction that the ongoing preservation of cultural specificity within this community is impossible." (Ibid., pp. 299–300)

96 Stalin, *Marxism and the National Question*, Chapter VII: "The National Question in Russia". On the debates among Marxists on the Jewish Question, see Enzo Traverso, *The Marxists and the Jewish Question: The History of a Debate (1843–1943)*, trans. Bernard Gibbons, Atlantic Highlands, NJ: Humanities Press, 1994.

97 Vladimir I. Lenin, "The Socialist Revolution and the Right of Nations to Self-Determination" [1916] (MIA, www.marxists.org/archive/lenin/works/1916/jan/x01. htm), § 3: "The Meaning of the Right to Self-Determination and its Relation to Federation". Eric Hobsbawm seems to have overlooked the dialectical dimension of Lenin's approach to the national question in his critique of this approach from a cosmopolitan perspective in the last chapter of his book on nationalism, *Nations and Nationalism since 1780: Programme, Myth, Reality*, 2d ed., Cambridge: Cambridge University Press, 1992.

98 Joseph Stalin, "The National Question and Leninism" [1929] (MIA, www.marxists. org/reference/archive/stalin/works/1929/03/18.htm), Chapter 2: "The Rise and Development of Nations."

99 Ibid.

100 Ibid., Chapter 3: "The Future of Nations and of National Languages". The same theme was reasserted during the 16th Congress of the CPSU (B) in 1930 (see Stalin's "Political Report of the Central Committee to the Sixteenth Congress of the C.P.S.U.(B.)" (www.marxists.org/reference/archive/stalin/works/1930/aug/27. htm), and his "Reply to the Discussion on the Political Report of the Central Committee to the Sixteenth Congress of the C.P.S.U.(B.)" (www.marxists.org/ reference/archive/stalin/works/1930/07/02.htm).

101 Quoted in V. Kubálková and A. Cruickshank, *Marxism–Leninism and Theory of International Relations*, London: Routledge & Kegan Paul, 1980, p. 139.

102 See Isaac Deutscher, *Stalin: A Political Biography*, 2nd edn, New York: Oxford University Press, 1967, pp. 487–93.

103 Leszek Kolakowski, *Main Currents of Marxism*, New York: W. W. Norton, 2008, p. 903.

104 Deutscher, *Stalin*, pp. 604–9.

105 Ibid., p. 607.

106 Ibid., p. 608.

107 F. Chernov, "Bourgeois Cosmopolitanism and its Reactionary Role" [1949] (available in English and in the Russian original on the Internet: www.cyberussr. com/rus/chernov/chernov-cosmo-e.html).

108 Ibid., § 1, "Cosmopolitanism infiltrates Soviet arts, sciences, history".

109 Ibid., § 3, "The worldwide struggle against 'cosmopolitan' imperialism".

110 Ibid., § 4, "Soviet Patriotism – a new and higher type." Another example of the Stalinist anti-cosmopolitan campaign is the 1950 book by Georges Cogniot, one of the most prominent historical leaders of the French Communist Party, *Réalité de la nation. L'attrape-nigaud du cosmopolitisme* (Paris: Editions sociales, 1950); see Michael Löwy's discussion of this work in "Marx & Engels: Cosmopolites", *Critique*, no. 14, 1981, pp. 5–12; repr. in Bob Jessop with Russell Wheatley, eds, *Karl Marx's Social and Political Thought, Vol. VII, The State, Politics, and Civil Society*, London: Routledge, 1999, pp. 248–9.

111 Kolakowski, *Main Currents of Marxism*, p. 908.

112 Howard Fast, "Cosmopolitanism" [1956] (available on the Internet at: www.trussel. com/hf/cosmopol.htm).

113 Natan Sznaider, "Hannah Arendt's Jewish Cosmopolitanism: Between the Universal and the Particular", *European Journal of Social Theory*, vol. 10, no. 1, 2007, p. 120.

114 Hannah Arendt, "Karl Jaspers: Citizen of the World?" [1957], in idem, *Men in Dark Times*, San Diego: Harcourt Brace, 1995, pp. 81–2. On Arendt's conception of cosmopolitanism, see Annabel Herzog, "Political Itineraries and Anarchic Cosmopolitanism in the Thought of Hannah Arendt", *Inquiry*, no. 47, 2004, pp. 20–41; on the debate between Arendt and Jaspers, see Seyla Benhabib, *Another Cosmopolitanism*, Robert Post, ed., with commentaries by Jeremy Waldron, Bonnie Honig, and Will Kymlicka, New York: Oxford University Press, 2006.

115 Ibid., p. 15.
116 Hannah Arendt, *Eichmann in Jerusalem: A Report on the Banality of Evil*, New York: Penguin, 1994, p. 298. On this issue as part of Arendt's "critical cosmopolitanism", see Robert Fine, "Arendt's Critical Cosmopolitanism", ch. 9 of idem, *Political Investigations: Hegel, Marx and Arendt*, London: Routledge, 2001, pp. 151–65.
117 Ernst Bloch, *The Principle of Hope*, Cambridge, MA: MIT Press, 1995, vol. II, pp. 896–7.
118 Ibid., p. 895.
119 Ibid., p. 897.
120 On the "new cosmopolitanism" see Robert Fine, *Cosmopolitanism*, Oxon: Routledge, 2007.
121 Peter Gowan, "The New Liberal Cosmopolitanism", *New Left Review*, II/11, Sept/Oct 2001, pp. 79–93 [repr. in Daniele Archibugi, ed., *Debating Cosmopolitics*, London: Verso, 2003, pp. 51–66].
122 Ibid., pp. 79–80. For a more pretentious version of this "new liberal cosmopolitanism", upholding "the experience of the Western Alliance and the European Union", see Ulrich Beck, *Cosmopolitan Vision*, Cambridge, UK: Polity, 2006. The standard left-wing ultra-cosmopolitan theorisation of the new capitalist cosmopolitanism as an established fact, halfway between the world-governmental perspective and the "new liberal" international regime, is, of course, Michael Hardt and Antonio Negri, *Empire*, Cambridge: Harvard University Press, 2000. The authors also believe that "globalization" renders "proletarian internationalism" obsolete (pp. 49–52).
123 Nadia Urbinati, "Can Cosmopolitical Democracy Be Democratic?", in Archibugi, ed., *Debating Cosmopolitics*, pp. 67–85.
124 See, among other works, the relevant essays collected in Jürgen Habermas, *The Inclusion of the Other: Studies in Political Theory*, Ciaran Cronin and Pablo De Greiff, eds, Cambridge, MA: MIT Press, 1998 – in particular the one written for the bicentenary of Kant's famous pamphlet: "Kant's Idea of Perpetual Peace: At Two Hundred Year's Historical Remove", pp. 165–201.
125 See, in particular, Daniele Archibugi and David Held, eds, *Cosmopolitan Democracy: An Agenda for a New World Order*, Cambridge, UK: Polity Press, 1995, and Daniele Archibugi, "Cosmopolitical Democracy", *New Left Review*, II/4, Jul/Aug 2000, pp. 137–150 [rpt. in Archibugi, ed., *Debating Cosmopolitics*, pp. 1–15].
126 See, in particular, Boaventura de Sousa Santos and César A. Rodríguez-Garavito, *Law and Globalization from Below: Towards a Cosmopolitan Legality*, Cambridge: Cambridge University Press, 2005.
127 See in particular Etienne Balibar, "Historical Dilemmas of Democracy and Their Contemporary Relevance for Citizenship", *Rethinking Marxism*, vol. 20, no. 4, 2008, pp. 522–38; Marie-Claire Caloz-Tschopp, *Les étrangers aux frontières de l'Europe et le spectre des camps*, Paris: La Dispute, 2004 and Sandro Mezzadra, *Diritto di fuga. Migrazioni, cittadinanza, globalizzazione*, Verona: Ombre corte, 2006.
128 Archibugi, "Cosmopolitical Democracy", p. 149.
129 Craig Calhoun, "The Class Consciousness of Frequent Travellers: Towards a Critique of Actually Existing Cosmopolitanism", in Archibugi, ed., *Debating*

Cosmopolitics, p. 112. "It is also disingenuous, if would-be cosmopolitans don't recognize the extent to which cosmopolitan appreciation of global diversity is based on privileges of wealth and perhaps especially citizenship in certain states." (Ibid.).

130 Gowan, "The New Liberal Cosmopolitanism", p. 93.

131 Daniele Archibugi, "Cosmopolitan Democracy and its Critics: A Review", *European Journal of International Relations*, vol. 10, no. 3, p. 466.

132 Urbinati, "Can Cosmopolitical Democracy Be Democratic?", p. 67.

133 Timothy Brennan, "Cosmopolitanism and Internationalism", *New Left Review*, II/7, Jan/Feb 2001, p. 84 [repr. in Archibugi, ed., *Debating Cosmopolitics*, pp. 40–50].

134 Ibid.

135 Pheng Cheah, "Given Culture: Rethinking Cosmopolitical Freedom in Transnationalism", in Cheah and Robins, eds, *Cosmopolitics: Thinking and Feeling beyond the Nation*, Minneapolis: University of Minnesota Press, 1998, p. 316. Pheng Cheah believes that postcolonial nationalism disproved Marx's "economism": Marx's thinking indeed went through such an initial phase, but managed to supersede it. The problem with many critics of Marx is that they do not consider the overall dynamic of his thought, and especially its most mature stage.

136 See Martha Nussbaum's essay "Patriotism and Cosmopolitanism" in the *Boston Review* (Sept/Oct 1994) and the debate around it, published in idem, *For Love of Country?: Debating the Limits of Patriotism*, ed. by Joshua Cohen, with respondents, Boston: Beacon Press, 1996.

137 Francis Fukuyama's review of Nussbaum's *For Love of Country?* in *Foreign Affairs*, vol. 76, no. 2, March/April 1997, p. 173. The resemblance between this criticism and the Stalinist one, as well as that expressed in some postcolonial nationalist circles, is striking.

138 Daniele Conversi, "Cosmopolitanism and Nationalism", in Athena Leoussi, ed., *Encyclopaedia of Nationalism*, New Brunswick: Transaction, 2000, p. 39.

139 An example of this is the dialectic between the defence of national gains and the fight for their extension to the European Union – the fight for a "European social state" – that Pierre Bourdieu advocated for Europe as an instance of the "new internationalism", in "For a New Internationalism" in idem, *Acts of Resistance: Against the New Myths of Our Time*, Cambridge, UK: Polity, 1998, pp. 60-69.

140 Boaventura de Sousa Santos, "Globalizations", *Theory, Culture & Society*, vol. 23, no. 2–3, 2006, p. 397.

141 Ibid., p. 398.

142 This is why many of the organisers of the World Social Forum insisted on replacing the label "anti-globalist" that the media stuck on them with "alter-globalist".

143 Bloch, *The Principle of Hope*, vol. III, p. 1375–6.

Bibliography and References

In the following, MECW refers to Karl Marx and Frederick Engels, *Collected Works*; MEW to Karl Marx and Friedrich Engels, *Werke*; and MIA to Marxists Internet Archive (see below for references). Thanks are due to Sebastian Budgen for facilitating my access to the MECW.

Abdel-Malek, Anouar, "Orientalism in crisis", *Diogenes*, vol. 11, no. 44, 1963, pp. 103–40; an excerpt from this article can be found in Macfie, ed., *Orientalism: A Reader*, pp. 47–56.

Achcar, Gilbert, "Engels: theorist of war, theorist of revolution", *International Socialism*, no. 97, Winter 2002, pp. 69–89; <http://pubs.socialistreviewindex. org.uk/isj97/achcar.htm>.

—, "Marx et Engels face à la guerre", in Arnaud Spire, ed., *Marx contemporain*, Paris: Syllepse, 2003, pp. 171–84.

—, *Eastern Cauldron: Islam, Afghanistan, Palestine and Iraq in a Marxist Mirror*, trans. Peter Drucker, New York: Monthly Review Press and London: Pluto Press, 2004.

—, "Marxists and Religion – Yesterday and Today", trans. Peter Cooper, first posted on *International Viewpoint*, 16 March 2005, <http:// internationalviewpoint.org/spip.php?article622>.

—, *The Clash of Barbarisms: The Making of the New World Disorder*, 2nd aug. edn, trans. Peter Drucker, Boulder, CO: Paradigm Publishers and London: Saqi, 2006.

—, with Michel Warschawski, *The 33-Day War: Israel's War on Hezbollah in Lebanon and Its Aftermath*, Boulder, CO: Paradigm Publishers and London: Saqi, 2007.

—, with Noam Chomsky, *Perilous Power: The Middle East and U.S. Foreign Policy*, Stephen Shalom, ed., Boulder, CO: Paradigm Publishers and London: Hamish Hamilton, 2007 (2nd exp. edn, Boulder, CO: Paradigm Publishers, 2009).

Afary, Janet and Kevin B. Anderson, *Foucault and the Iranian Revolution: Gender and the Seductions of Islamism*, Chicago: The University of Chicago Press, 2005.

Ahmad, Aijaz, *In Theory: Classes, Nations, Literatures*, London: Verso, 1992.

A.I.T., *L'Alliance de la Démocratie Socialiste et l'Association Internationale des Travailleurs. Rapport et documents publiés par ordre du Congrès International de la Haye*, London: A. Darson, 1873.

Alighieri, Dante, *De Monarchia* [ca. 1312], trans. Aurelia Henry (1904), <http://oll.libertyfund.org/index.php?option=com_staticxt&staticfile=show.php%3Ftitle=2196&Itemid=27>.

Althusser, Louis, *For Marx*, trans. Ben Brewster, Harmondsworth, UK: Penguin, 1969.

—, *Lenin and Philosophy and Other Essays*, trans. Ben Brewster, London: New Left Books, 1971.

'Amil, Mahdi, *Hal al-qalb lil-sharq wal-'aql lil-gharb? Marx fi Istishraq Edward Said*, Beirut: Al-Farabi, 1985.

Amin, Samir, *Eurocentrism*, trans. R. Moore and J. Membrez, New York: Monthly Review Press, 1989.

Anderson, Kevin, *Marx at the Margins: On Nationalism, Ethnicity, and Non-Western Societies*, Chicago: University of Chicago Press, 2010.

Archibugi, Daniele, "Cosmopolitical Democracy", *New Left Review*, II/4, Jul/Aug 2000, pp. 137–50; repr. in Archibugi, ed., pp. 1–15.

— ed., *Debating Cosmopolitics*, London: Verso, 2003.

—, "Cosmopolitan Democracy and its Critics: A Review", *European Journal of International Relations*, vol. 10, no. 3, 2004, pp. 437–73.

Archibugi, Daniele and David Held, eds (1995), *Cosmopolitan Democracy: An Agenda for a New World Order*, Cambridge, UK: Polity Press.

Arendt, Hannah, *Eichmann in Jerusalem: A Report on the Banality of Evil*, New York: Penguin, 1994.

—, "Karl Jaspers: Citizen of the World?" [1957], in idem, *Men in Dark Times*, San Diego: Harcourt Brace, 1995, pp. 81–94.

Al-'Azm, Sadik [Sadiq] Jalal, *Al-istishraq wal-istishraq maakusan*, Beirut: Dar al-Hadatha, 1981.

—, "Orientalism and Orientalism in Reverse", *Khamsin 8*, London: Ithaca Press, 1981, pp. 5–26; repr. in A. L. Macfie, ed., *Orientalism: A Reader*, pp. 217–38.

—, "Islamic Fundamentalism Reconsidered: A Critical Outline of Problems, Ideas and Approaches", Part I and II, in *South Asia Bulletin*, vol. XIII, no. 1&2, 1993, pp. 93–121, and vol. XIV, no. 1, 1994, pp. 73–98.

Balibar, Etienne, "Historical Dilemmas of Democracy and Their Contemporary Relevance for Citizenship", *Rethinking Marxism*, vol. 20, no. 4, 2008, pp. 522–38.

Bauer, Otto, *The Question of Nationalities and Social Democracy* [orig. published in German in 1907], trans. Joseph O'Donnell, Minneapolis: University of

Minnesota Press, 2000.

Bax, Ernest Belfort, *The Peasants War in Germany 1525–1526*, London: Swan Sonnenschein & Co, 1899.

Beck, Ulrich, *Cosmopolitan Vision*, Cambridge, UK: Polity Press, 2006.

Benhabib, Seyla, *Another Cosmopolitanism*, ed. by Robert Post with commentaries by Jeremy Waldron, Bonnie Honig, and Will Kymlicka, New York: Oxford University Press, 2006.

Bensaïd, Daniel, ed., *Karl Marx, Sur la Question Juive. Présentation et commentaires de Daniel Bensaïd*, Paris: Textuel, 2006.

Bevilacqua, Alexander, "Conceiving the Republic of Mankind: The Political Thought of Anacharsis Cloots", *History of European Ideas*, vol. 38, no. 4, December 2012, pp. 550–69.

Bloch, Ernst, *Thomas Münzer als Theologe der Revolution*, Leipzig: Reclam, 1989.

—, *The Principle of Hope*, 3 vols [orig. published in German in 1938–1947], Cambridge, MA: MIT Press, 1995.

Bourdieu, Pierre, "For a New Internationalism", in idem, *Acts of Resistance: Against the New Myths of Our Time*, Cambridge, UK: Polity, 1998, pp. 60–9.

Brennan, Timothy, "Cosmopolitanism and Internationalism", *New Left Review*, II/7, Jan/Feb 2001, pp. 75–84; repr. in Archibugi, ed., pp. 40–50.

Brière, Claire and Pierre Blanchet, *Iran: La révolution au nom de Dieu*, Paris: Seuil, 1979.

Brière, Claire and Olivier Carré, *Islam: Guerre à l'Occident ?*, Paris: Autrement, 1983.

Burgat, François, *L'islamisme au Maghreb: La voix du Sud*, Paris: Karthala, 1988; English translation, Burgat with William Dowell.

—, "De la difficulté de nommer: *intégrisme, fondamentalisme, islamisme*", *Les Temps modernes*, March 1988, pp. 119–39.

—, *L'islamisme en face*, Paris: La Découverte, 1995; English translation: *Face to Face with Political Islam*, London: I. B. Tauris, 2003.

—, *L'islamisme à l'heure d'Al-Qaida*, Paris: La Découverte, 2005.

Burgat, François, with William Dowell, *The Islamic Movement in North Africa*, Austin: University of Texas, 1992.

Busch, H. J. and A. Horstmann, "Kosmopolit, Kosmopolitismus. 1." in Joachim Ritter, Karlfried Gründer and Gottfried Gabriel, eds, *Historisches Wörterbuch der Philosophie*, vol. 4, Basel: Schwabe Verlag, 1976, pp. 1155–8.

Calhoun, Craig, "The Class Consciousness of Frequent Travellers: Towards a Critique of Actually Existing Cosmopolitanism", in Archibugi, ed., pp. 87–116.

Caloz-Tschopp, Marie-Claire, *Les étrangers aux frontières de l'Europe et le spectre des camps*, Paris: La Dispute, 2004.

Carré, Olivier, *La légitimation islamique des socialismes arabes. Analyse conceptuelle combinatoire des manuels scolaires égyptiens, syriens et irakiens*, Paris: FNSP, 1979.

—, ed., *L'Islam et l'Etat dans le monde d'aujourd'hui*, Paris: PUF, 1982.

—, *L'Utopie islamique dans l'Orient arabe*, Paris: FNSP, 1991.

—, *L'Islam laïque ou le retour à la Grande Tradition*, Paris: Armand Colin, 1993.

Carré, Olivier and Michel Seurat [using the pseudonym of Gérard Michaud], ed., *Les Frères musulmans Égypte et Syrie (1928–1982)*, Paris: Gallimard/ Julliard, 1983.

Chandra, Bipan, "Karl Marx, His Theories of Asian Societies and Colonial Rule", in UNESCO, ed., *Sociological Theories: Race and Colonialism*, Paris: Unesco, 1980, pp. 383–451.

Cheah, Pheng, "Given Culture: Rethinking Cosmopolitical Freedom in Transnationalism", in Pheng Cheah and Bruce Robins, eds, *Cosmopolitics: Thinking and Feeling beyond the Nation*, Minneapolis: University of Minnesota Press, 1998, pp. 290–328.

—, "Cosmopolitanism", *Theory, Culture & Society*, vol. 23, no. 2–3, 2006, pp. 486–96.

Chernov, F., "Bourgeois Cosmopolitanism and its Reactionary Role", orig. published in Russian in 1949, <http://www.cyberussr.com/rus/chernov/ chernov-cosmo-e.html>.

Clément, Jean-François, "Pour une compréhension des mouvements islamistes", *Esprit*, January 1980, pp. 38–51.

Cloots, Anacharsis, *La République Universelle ou Adresse aux tyrannicides*, orig. published in 1792, French text available on the Internet from various websites.

Cogniot, Georges, *Réalité de la nation. L'attrape-nigaud du cosmopolitisme*, Paris: Editions sociales, 1950.

Conversi, Daniele, "Cosmopolitanism and Nationalism", in Athena Leoussi, ed., *Encyclopaedia of Nationalism*, New Brunswick: Transaction, 2000, pp. 34–9.

Degras, Jane, ed., *The Communist International 1919–1943: Documents*, vol. I (1919–1922), London: Oxford University Press, 1956.

—, *The Communist International 1919–1943: Documents*, vol. II (1923–1928), London: Oxford University Press, 1960.

—, *The Communist International 1919–1943: Documents*, vol. III (1929–1943), London: Oxford University Press, 1965.

Deutscher, Isaac, *Stalin: A Political Biography*, 2nd edn, New York: Oxford University Press, 1967.

Engels, Frederick [Friedrich] (F. Oswald), "Ernst Moritz Arndt" (*Telegraph für Deutschland*, no. 2–5, January 1841), MECW, vol. 2, p. 137–50.

—, *Outlines of a Critique of Political Economy*, MECW, vol. 3, pp. 418–43.

—, "Rapid Progress of Communism in Germany" (*The New Moral World*, no. 25, 13 December 1844), MECW, vol. 4, p. 229–33.

—, "The Festival of Nations in London", MECW, vol. 6, pp. 3–14.

—, "Reform Movement in France – Banquet of Dijon" (*Northern Star*, December 18, 1847), vol. 6, pp. 397–401.

—, "Extraordinary Revelations. – Abd-El-Kader. – Guizot's Foreign Policy", MECW, vol. 6, p. 469–72.

—, *Der deutsche Bauernkrieg*, MEW (see below, Marx, Karl and Friedrich Engels), vol. 7, pp. 327–413.

—, *The Peasant War in Germany*, MECW, vol. 10, pp. 397–482.

—, "Algeria", *Articles for The New American Cyclopaedia*, MECW, vol. 18, p. 60–70.

—, *Ludwig Feuerbach and the End of Classical German Philosophy*, MECW, vol. 26, pp. 353–98.

—, "On the History of Early Christianity", in MECW, vol. 27, pp. 445–69.

—, "Frederick Engels to Friedrich Adolph Sorge" (12[–17] Sept. 1874), MECW, vol. 45, pp. 40–4.

—, *Anti-Dühring: Herr Eugen Dühring's Revolution in Science*, MECW, vol. 25, pp. 1–309.

Fast, Howard, "Cosmopolitanism", orig. published in 1956, <http://www.trussel.com/hf/cosmopol.htm>.

Fine, Robert, "Arendt's Critical Cosmopolitanism", in idem, *Political Investigations: Hegel, Marx and Arendt*, London: Routledge, 2001, pp. 151–65.

—, *Cosmopolitanism*, Oxon: Routledge, 2007.

Foucault, Michel, *The Order of Things: An Archaeology of the Human Sciences*, London: Tavistock, 1970.

—, *Dits et écrits II, 1976–1988*, Paris: Gallimard, 2001.

Fukuyama, Francis, "Review of *For Love of Country: Debating the Limits of Patriotism* by Martha C. Nussbaum", *Foreign Affairs*, vol. 76, no. 2 (Mar. - Apr., 1997), p. 173.

Gallissot, René, *Marx, Marxisme et Algérie. Textes de Marx-Engels*, introduced and translated by René Gallissot in collaboration with Gilbert Badia, Paris: UGE 10/18, 1976.

Gowan, Peter, "The New Liberal Cosmopolitanism", *New Left Review*, II/11, Sept/Oct 2001, pp. 79–93; repr. in Archibugi, ed., 2003, pp. 51–66.

Gramsci, Antonio (1977), *Quaderni del carcere, Edizione critica dell'Istituto Gramsci*, 4 vols, 2nd edn, Turin: Einaudi.

—, *Prison Notebooks*, 3 vols, edited and translated by Joseph A. Buttigieg, with Antonio Callari for vol. I, New York: Columbia University Press, 1992, 1996, 2007.

Habermas, Jürgen, *The Inclusion of the Other: Studies in Political Theory*, ed. Ciaran Cronin and Pablo De Greiff, trans. Ciaran Cronin, Cambridge, MA: MIT Press, 1998.

Hardt, Michael and Antonio Negri, *Empire*, Cambridge: Harvard University

Press, 2000.

Haupt, Georges, Michael Löwy, and Claudie Weill, *Les marxistes et la question nationale*, Paris: François Maspero, 1974.

Hegel, G. W. F., *The Philosophy of History*, trans. J. Sibree, New York: Dover Publications, 1956.

Herzog, Annabel, "Political Itineraries and Anarchic Cosmopolitanism in the Thought of Hannah Arendt", *Inquiry*, no. 47, 2004, pp. 20–41.

Hobsbawm, E. J., *Nations and Nationalism since 1780: Programme, Myth, Reality*, 2nd edn, Cambridge: Cambridge University Press, 1992.

Hocquenghem, Guy, *Lettre ouverte à ceux qui sont passés du col Mao au Rotary* [1986], Marseille: Agone, 2003, preface by Serge Halimi.

Hopkins, Nicholas S., "Engels and Ibn Khaldun", *Alif: Journal of Comparative Poetics*, American University in Cairo, no. 10, 1990, pp. 9–18.

Howe, Stephen, "Edward Said and Marxism: Anxieties of Influence", *Cultural Critique*, no. 67, Fall 2007, pp. 50–87.

Jessop, Bob, with Russell Wheatley, *Karl Marx's Social and Political Thought*, vol. VII, *The State, Politics, and Civil Society*, London: Routledge, 1999.

Kant, Immanuel, *The Metaphysics of Morals* [orig. published in German in 1797], trans. and ed. by Mary Gregor, Cambridge: Cambridge University Press, 1996.

——, *Perpetual Peace: A Philosophical Sketch* [orig. published in German in 1795], different translations available on the Internet from various websites.

Kautsky, Karl, *Thomas More and his Utopia* [orig. published in German in 1888], trans. Henry James Stenning (1927), MIA, <https://www.marxists.org/archive/kautsky/1888/more/index.htm>.

—— (1908), *Foundations of Christianity* [orig. published in German in 1908], trans. Henry F. Mins (1953), MIA, <http://www.marxists.org/archive/kautsky/1908/christ/index.htm>.

Kepel, Gilles, *Le Prophète et Pharaon. Les mouvements islamistes dans l'Egypte contemporaine*, Paris: La Découverte, 1984; English translation: *The Prophet and Pharaoh: Muslim Extremism in Contemporary Egypt*, trans. Jon Rothschild, with a preface by Bernard Lewis, London: Saqi, 1985.

Khosrokhavar, Farhad, "Du néo-orientalisme de Badie: enjeux et méthodes", *Peuples méditerranéens*, no. 50, January–March 1990, pp. 121–48.

Kleingeld, Pauline and Eric Brown, "Cosmopolitanism", in Edward N. Zalta, ed., *The Stanford Encyclopedia of Philosophy*, Winter 2006 Edition, <http://plato.stanford.edu/archives/win2006/entries/cosmopolitanism/>.

Kolakowski, Leszek, *Main Currents of Marxism*, New York: W. W. Norton, 2008.

Kouvelakis, Stathis, *Philosophy and Revolution: From Kant to Marx*, trans. G. M. Goshgarian, London: Verso, 2003.

Krader, Lawrence, *The Asiatic Mode of Production: Sources, Development and Critique in the Writings of Karl Marx*, Assen: Van Gorcum, 1975.

Kriwaczek, Paul, *Yiddish Civilisation: The Rise and Fall of a Forgotten Nation*, New York: Vintage Books, 2006.

Kubálková, V. and A. Cruickshank, *Marxism-Leninism and Theory of International Relations*, London: Routledge & Kegan Paul, 1980.

Laertius, Diogenes, *The Lives and Opinions of Eminent Philosophers*, trans. C. D. Yonge (1853), <http://classicpersuasion.org/pw/diogenes/>.

Lafargue, Paul, *Le déterminisme économique de Karl Marx. Recherches sur l'origine et l'évolution des idées de Justice, du Bien, de l'Âme et de Dieu*, 1909, Internet facsimile: Gallica/BNF, <http://gallica.bnf.fr/ark:/12148/bpt6k80118z. r=lafargue.langEN>.

Laroui, Abdallah, *L'idéologie arabe contemporaine*, preface by Maxime Rodinson, Paris: François Maspero, 1967.

Lenin, Vladimir I., "The Position of the Bund in the Party", 1903, Marxist Internet Archive, <http://www.marxists.org/archive/lenin/works/1903/ oct/22a.htm>.

—, "The Socialist Revolution and the Right of Nations to Self-Determination", 1916, Marxist Internet Archive, <http://www.marxists.org/archive/lenin/ works/1916/jan/x01.htm>.

Leon, Abram, *The Jewish Question: A Marxist Interpretation*, English translation 1950, Marxist Internet Archive, <http://www.marxists.org/subject/jewish/ leon/index.htm>.

Lindner, Kolja, "Marx's Eurocentrism: Postcolonial Studies and Marx Scholarship", *Radical Philosophy*, no. 161, May/June 2010, pp. 27–41.

List, Friedrich, *The National System of Political Economy* [orig. published in German in 1841], trans. Sampson Lloyd (1885), available on the Internet from various websites.

Löwy, Michael, "Le problème de l'histoire: Remarques de théorie et de méthode", in Haupt, Löwy, and Weill, *Les marxistes et la question nationale*, pp. 370–91.

—, *The War of Gods: Religion and Politics in Latin America*, London: Verso, 1996.

—, "Marx & Engels: Cosmopolites", *Critique*, no. 14, 1981, pp. 5–12; repr. in Jessop, 1999, pp. 245–55.

—, *The Theory of Revolution in the Young Marx*, Leiden: Brill, 2003; rept. Chicago: Haymarket, 2005.

Löwy, Michael and Robert Sayre, *Romanticism Against the Tide of Modernity*, trans. Catherine Porter, Durham, NC: Duke University Press, 2001.

Lu, Catherine, "World Government", in Edward N. Zalta, ed., *The Stanford Encyclopedia of Philosophy*, Fall 2008 Edition, <http://plato.stanford.edu/ archives/fall2008/entries/world-government/>.

Macfie, Alexander Lyon, ed., *Orientalism: A Reader*, New York: NYU Press, 2000.

—, *Orientalism*, Harlow: Pearson Education, 2002.

Marx, Karl, *On the Jewish Question*, MECW (see below, Marx, Karl and Frederick Engels), vol. 3, pp. 146–74.

—, *Zur Kritik der Hegelschen Rechtsphilosophie. Einleitung*, MEW, vol. 1, pp. 378–91.

—, *Critique of Hegel's "Philosophy of Right"*, ed. by Joseph O'Malley, trans. Annette Jolin and Joseph O'Malley, Cambridge, UK: Cambridge University Press, 1970.

—, *Contribution to the Critique of Hegel's Philosophy of Law. Introduction*, MECW, vol. 3, pp. 175–87.

—, *Economic and Philosophic Manuscripts of 1844*, MECW, vol. 3, pp. 229–346.

—, "Draft of an Article on Friedrich List's book: *Das Nationale System der Politischen Oekonomie*", MECW, vol. 4, pp. 265–93.

—, "Theses on Feuerbach", MECW, vol. 5, pp. 6–8.

—, "Speech on the Question of Free Trade", MECW, vol. 6, pp. 450–65.

—, *The Eighteenth Brumaire of Louis Bonaparte*, MECW, vol. 11, pp. 99–197.

—, "The British Rule in India", MECW, vol. 12, p. 125–33.

—, *Grundrisse der Kritik der politischen Ökonomie*, 2nd edn, Berlin: Dietz Verlag, 1974.

—, *Grundrisse*, MECW, vol. 28 and 29 (pp. 3–255).

—, *A Contribution to the Critique of Political Economy. Preface*, MECW, vol. 29, pp. 257–65.

—, *Capital Volume I*, MECW, vol. 35.

—, "Afterword" to the Second German Edition of *Das Kapital*, MECW, vol. 35, p. 12–20.

—, "First Address of the General Council of the International Working Men's Association on the Franco–Prussian War", MECW, vol. 22, pp. 3–8.

—, "Second Address of the General Council of the International Working Men's Association on the Franco–Prussian War", MECW, vol. 22, pp. 263–70.

—, *The Civil War in France. Address of the General Council of the International Working Men's Association*, MECW, vol. 22, pp. 307–59.

—, *The First International and After*, ed. by David Fernbach, Harmondsworth: Penguin, in association with *New Left Review*, 1974.

—, *Marginal Notes on the Programme of the German Workers' Party*, MECW, vol. 24, pp. 81–99.

—, Karl Marx, Excerpts from M. M. Kovalevskij (Kovalevsky), *Obščinnoe Zemlevladenie*, in Krader, *The Asiatic Mode of Production*, pp. 343–412.

—, "Drafts of the Letter to Vera Zasulich" and "Letter to Vera Zasulich", MECW, vol. 24, pp. 346–71.

—, "Marx to Ferdinand Lassalle" (22 February 1858), MECW, vol. 40, pp 268–70.

Marx, Karl and Frederick [Friedrich] Engels, *Werke* (MEW), vol. 1–39 and Ergänzungsband 1–2, Berlin, Dietz Verlag, 1956–1968.

—, *Collected Works* (MECW), vol. 1–47, London: Lawrence and Wishart, 1970–2002.

—, *The Holy Family or Critique of Critical Criticism: Against Bruno Bauer and Company*, MECW, vol. 4, pp. 3–211.

—, *The German Ideology*, MECW, vol. 5.

—, *Manifesto of the Communist Party*, MECW, vol. 6, pp. 477–519.

—, *The Alliance of Socialist Democracy and the International Working Men's Association*, MECW, vol. 23, pp. 454–580.

—, "For Poland", MECW, vol. 24, pp. 55–8.

Marxists Internet Archive (MIA), <http://www.marxists.org/>.

Mayer, Anton, *Der zensierte Jesus: Soziologie des Neuen Testament*, Olten: Walter Verlag, 1983.

Meddeb, Abdelwahab, *The Malady of Islam*, trans. Pierre Joris and Ann Reid, New York: Basic Books, 2003.

Mehring, Franz, *Karl Marx: The Story of His Life* [orig. published in German in 1918], trans. Edward Fizgerald (1935), <http://www.marxists.org/archive/mehring/1918/marx/index.htm>.

Mezzadra, Sandro, *Diritto di fuga. Migrazioni, cittadinanza, globalizzazione*, Verona: Ombre corte, 2006.

Mill, John Stuart, *The Principles of Political Economy with Some of their Applications to Social Philosophy* [1848], available on the Internet from various websites.

Mommsen, Theodor, *The History of Rome*, vol. 1–5 [orig. published in German in 1854–1856], trans. William P. Dickson (1870), Internet edition: Project Gutenberg, <http://www.gutenberg.org/ebooks/10706>.

Nussbaum, Martha, *For Love of Country?: Debating the Limits of Patriotism*, ed. by Joshua Cohen, with respondents, Boston: Beacon Press, 1996.

Proto, Maria, ed., *Gramsci e l'Internazionalismo*, Manduria-Bari-Roma: Piero Lacaita Editore, 1967.

Rodinson, Maxime, "The Western Image and Western Studies of Islam", in Joseph Schacht with C. E. Bosworth, *The Legacy of Islam*, 2nd edn, Oxford: Clarendon Press, 1974, pp. 9–62.

—, *Islam and Capitalism*, trans. Brian Pearce, London: Allen Lane, 1974; repr. London: Saqi Books, 2007.

—, *La Fascination de l'Islam*, Paris: Maspero, 1980, p. 100; English translation: *Europe and the Mystique of Islam*, trans. Roger Veinus, Seattle: University of Washington Press, 1987 and London: I.B. Tauris, 1988.

—, *L'Islam: politique et croyance*, Paris: Fayard, 1993.

—, "Fantôme et réalités de l'orientalisme'", *Qantara*, no. 13, Oct.–Dec. 1994, pp. 27–30.

—, "Maxime Rodinson on Islamic Fundamentalism: An Unpublished Interview with Gilbert Achcar", in *Middle East Report*, Washington, no. 233, Winter

2004, pp. 2–4.

Rosdolsky, Roman, "The Workers and the Fatherland: A Note on a Passage in the *Communist Manifesto*", *Science and Society*, vol. 29, no. 3, 1965, pp. 330–7, <http://www.marxists.org/archive/rosdolsky/1965/workers.htm>.

—, "The Neue Rheinische Zeitung and the Jews", appendix of *Engels and the "Nonhistoric" Peoples: The National Question in the Revolution of 1848*, trans. and ed. by John-Paul Himka, *Critique: Journal of Socialist Theory*, vol. 18, no. 1, 1991, pp. 191–207.

Roy, Olivier, *L'Afghanistan. Islam et modernité politique*, Paris: Seuil, 1985; English translation: *Islam and Resistance in Afghanistan*, trans. First Edition, Cambridge, UK: Cambridge University Press, 1986.

—, *L'Échec de l'Islam politique*, Paris: Seuil, 1992; English translation: *The Failure of Political Islam*, trans. Carol Volk, Cambridge, MA: Harvard University Press, 1994.

—, "Les islamologues ont-ils inventé l'islamisme?", *Esprit*, August–September 2001, pp. 116–36.

—, *L'islam mondialisé*, Paris: Seuil, 2002; English edition, *Globalised Islam: The Search for a New Ummah*, London: Hurst & Co., 2004.

—, "Why Do They Hate Us? Not Because of Iraq", *New York Times*, 22 July 2005.

—, "L'Iran fait monter les enchères", *Le Monde*, 21 July 2006.

—, "We're winning, despite the 'war'", *International Herald Tribune*, 7 September 2006.

Said, Edward, "Orientalism Reconsidered", *Cultural Critique*, no. 1, Autumn 1985, pp. 89–107.

—, "Entretien avec Edward Said. Propos recueillis par Hassan Arfaoui et Subhi Hadidi", *M.A.R.S.*, no. 4, Winter 1995, pp. 7–22.

—, *Orientalism*, 25th Anniversary Edition with a New Preface by the Author, New York: Vintage Books, 2003.

Sand, Shlomo, *The Invention of the Jewish People*, trans. Yael Lotan, London: Verso, 2009.

—, *The Invention of the Land of Israel: From Holy Land to Homeland*, trans. Geremy Forman, London: Verso, 2012.

Santos, Boaventura de Sousa, "Globalizations", *Theory, Culture & Society*, vol. 23, no. 2–3, 2006, pp. 393–9.

Santos, Boaventura de Sousa and César A. Rodríguez-Garavito, *Law and Globalization from Below: Towards a Cosmopolitan Legality*, Cambridge: Cambridge University Press, 2005.

Seurat, Michel, *L'État de barbarie*, Paris: Seuil, 1989.

Siegel, Paul N., *The Meek and the Militant: Religion and Power Across the World*, London: Zed Press, 1986 (rept. Chicago: Haymarket, 2004).

Smith, Adam, *An Inquiry into the Nature and Causes of the Wealth of Nations*

[1776], available on the Internet from various websites.

Stalin, Joseph V., *Marxism and the National Question* [orig. published in Russian in 1913], MIA, <http://www.marxists.org/reference/archive/stalin/works/1913/03a.htm>.

—, "The National Question and Leninism" [1929], MIA, <http://www.marxists.org/reference/archive/stalin/works/1929/03/18.htm>.

—, "Political Report of the Central Committee to the Sixteenth Congress of the C.P.S.U.(B.)" [1930], <http://www.marxists.org/reference/archive/stalin/works/1930/aug/27.htm>.

—, "Reply to the Discussion on the Political Report of the Central Committee to the Sixteenth Congress of the C.P.S.U.(B.)" [1930], <http://www.marxists.org/reference/archive/stalin/works/1930/07/02.htm>).

Sznaider, Natan, "Hannah Arendt's Jewish Cosmopolitanism: Between the Universal and the Particular", *European Journal of Social Theory*, vol. 10, no. 1, 2007, pp. 112–22.

Thompson, Brian, "The 21st Century Will Be Religious or Will Not Be: Malraux's Controversial Dictum", in *André Malraux Review*, vol. 30, no. 1/2, 2001, pp. 110–23.

Thorner, Daniel, "Marx on India and the Asiatic Mode of Production", *Contributions to Indian Sociology*, no. 9, December 1966, pp. 33–66.

Toscano, Alberto, *Fanaticism: On the Uses of an Idea*, London: Verso, 2010.

Traverso, Enzo, *The Marxists and the Jewish Question: The History of a Debate (1843–1943)*, trans. Bernard Gibbons, Atlantic Highlands, NJ: Humanities Press, 1993.

Turner, Bryan, *Marx and the End of Orientalism*, London: George Allen & Unwin, 1978.

Urbinati, Nadia, "Can Cosmopolitical Democracy Be Democratic?", in Archibugi, ed., pp. 67–85.

Van der Linden, Marcel, "Labour Internationalism", in idem. *Workers of the World: Essays Toward a Global Labor History*, Leiden: Brill, 2008, pp. 259–83.

Weber, Max, *Economy and Society*, ed. by Guenther Roth and Claus Wittich, vol. 2, Berkeley: University of California Press, 1978.

Weinstock, Nathan, *Le pain de misère. Histoire du mouvement ouvrier juif en Europe*, vol. I, *L'empire russe jusqu'en 1914*, Paris: La découverte, 1984.

GILBERT ACHCAR is Professor at the School of Oriental and African Studies, University of London. His most recent book is *The People Want: A Radical Exploration of the Arab Uprising*. His other previous works include the highly acclaimed *The Arabs and the Holocaust: The Arab–Israeli War of Narratives*, *The Clash of Barbarisms: The Making of the New World Disorder* and, with Noam Chomsky, *Perilous Power: The Middle East and US Foreign Policy*.